D1453052

THE TORCH-BEARERS—III

THE
LAST VOYAGE

BY

ALFRED NOYES

NEW YORK
FREDERICK A. STOKES COMPANY
MCMXXX

DEDICATION
TO
MARY ANGELA

Under the Pyrenees,
  Where the warm sea-wind drifts thro' tama-
    risk boughs,
There is a lonely house upon a hill-top
That I shall never forget or see again.

I shall not see that garden, filled with roses,
  On the high sun-burnt plateau, girdled
    round
With that low parapet, on the lonely hill-top,
By sunlight, or by moonlight, ever again.

In that lost garden stands a little chapel,
  And the strange ship wherein we made our
    voyage,

[v]

Our little mortal ship of thoughts and visions,
Hangs there, in chains, before the twilit altar.
  The doors are locked. The lamp is quenched
    for ever;
Though, at one corner of the house, Our Lady
Looks out, across the valley, to the sea.

And, on the landward side, across a valley
  Purple as grapes in autumn, the dark moun-
    tains,
With peaks like broken swords, and splintered
    helmets,
    Remembering Roland's death, are listening
    still.

Look down, look down, upon the sunlit valley,
  Over the low white parapet of that garden;
And you shall see the long white road go
    winding
    Through the Basque vineyards. . . .
                        But you shall not see
One face, nor shall you hear one voice that
    whispered
    Love, as it died. . . .
                  Only one wooden Image
[vi]

Knows where she knelt, among the lonely mountains
At Roncesvalles, in one last prayer for me. . . .

*　　*　　*　　*　　*　　*　　*

AND, when it was darkest, I came to a
strong City.
No earthly tongue can tell how I journeyed
there,
Deaf to this world's compassion,
Blind to its pity,
With a heart wrung empty, even of its last
dumb prayer.

I had left the chattering throngs in the night
behind me,
And stumbled into a desert that had no name.
Torn, bleeding of foot,
Through cactus and thorn I stumbled,
And, when it was darkest, to that strong City
I came.

[vii]

Gate there was none, nor window. It towered
  above me
  Like a vast fortress into the midnight sky.
And I beat on the granite walls,
  But I found no doorway;
And the blood ran over my wrists, but I heard
  no reply.

Yet—I knew well—no tongue can tell how I
  knew it—
  Though the walls were harder than
  adamant, blacker than night,
Within that City
  Was glory beyond all glory
Of wisdom and power enthroned in absolute
  light.

Could I have entered there, all doubt were
  over.
  Stones would be bread at last, and water
  wine;
All questioning closed
      In absolute vision;
The long sad riddle solved, and the answer
  mine.

[viii]

But oh, on those cloud-wreathed walls, there
   stood no sentry.
Naked as cliffs they towered, abrupt as doom.
   No shining gateway,
     No shadowy postern,
No least small spark of a window broke their
   gloom.

Hour after hopeless hour I groped around
   them.
   League after league, I followed that gir-
   dling wall.
Burning with thirst,
I dragged through the drifted sand-heaps
   Round its great coigns, and found them
   adamant all.

Once, every league, a shadowy buttress
   Like a vast Sphinx, outstretched in the
   moon's pale sheen,
Loomed through the night,
With flanks worn sleek by the sand-storms,
   And calm strange face that gazed as at
   worlds unseen.

I groped around them; I groped around them;
  Stared up at their cold eyes and found them
    stone;
And crawled on, on,
Till I overtook strange foot-prints
  Going my way, and knew them for my own;

Strange foot-prints, clotted with blood, in the
    sand before me,
  Trailing the hopeless way I had trailed be-
    fore;
For, in that night,
I had girdled the whole dark City,
  Feeling each adamant inch, and found no
    door.

I fell on my face in the rank salt of the desert.
  Slow, hot, like blood, out of my hopeless
    eyes,
The salt tears bled.
The salt of the desert drank them,
  And I cried, once, to God, as a child cries.

Then, then, I cannot tell
What strange thing happened,

Only, as at a breath of the midnight air,
These eyes, like two staunched wounds, had
      ceased their bleeding
And my despair had ended my despair.

Far over the desert, like shadows trailed by a
      moon-cloud,
   I saw a train of mourners, two by two,
Following an open coffin.
   They halted near me.
And I beheld, once more, the face I knew.

Blissful the up-turned face—the cold hands
      folded,
   Blissful the up-turned face, cold as cold
      stone,
Cold as a midnight flower.
   I bent above it—
Sweet, sweet cold kiss, the saddest earth had
      known.

Quietly they moved on, in slow procession.
   They breathed no prayer. They sang no
      funeral song.
Up to the adamant walls
   Of that strong City,

Slowly they moved, a strange inscrutable
throng.

Behind their shining burden they stole like
shadows
Up to the shadowy City, two by two.
And like two ponderous doors of a tomb re-
volving
Two stones in the wall swung back,
And they passed through.

I followed after. I followed after.
Theirs was the secret key, and the sure goal:
And the adamant doors
Revolved again like midnight,
And closed, like a silent thunder, behind my
soul.

Dark! It was dark; but through that strange
new darkness
Great aisles of beauty rapturously burned;
And I stole on,
Like a remembering pilgrim
From a long exile now at last returned.

All round me burned strange lights and
    banners.
Above, great arches grasped and spanned
    the sky.
Then, like a bell,
    In the armoured hands of Michael,
I heard Time ring its æons out and die.

I saw that strange procession winding
    On through a veil that shielded my dazed
    sight
From the absolute Dark that would have
    drowned me
    At the first dreadful touch of absolute Light.

Yet I saw glory on glory on glory
    Burning through those ethereal folds
Dusked by a myriad dawns, a myriad sunsets
    With smouldering mercies, merciful blood-
    red golds.

Before it smoked the Eternal Altar
    Branched with great trembling lights that
    shone
As though at last all stars, all constellations,

Had swung to their true place before God's
throne.

There, there, at last, they burned in order,
Round that high Altar, under that rich East.
All clouds, all snows, on that pure Table
Were spread like one white cloth for God's
own feast.

And I heard *Sanctus, Sanctus, Sanctus,*
Dominus Deus, echoing everywhere,
In tongues of earth, in tongues of ocean,
In tongues of fire, in tongues of air.

Far off, I heard once more the centuries peal-
ing
Like one brief sacring bell, I heard Time
die.
I saw Space fading, forms dissolving,
I saw the Host uplifted high.

Spirit and Substance, Victim-Victor,
One life in all, all lives in One,
Fast-bound to feed man's bounded vision
Shone through that strict concentering Sun.

Anima Mundi, World-Sustainer
   Sower to whom all seeds returned,
Through earth's dissolving mist of atoms
   The Body of God in splendour burned.

And I heard *Agnus, Agnus Dei,*
   Pleading for man with Love's own breath;
And Love drew near me,
   And Love drew near me
And I drank Life through God's own death.

THE LAST VOYAGE

PRELUDE

THE mist rolled back.
　　There was a roar of waters;
And it was night, black night, in midmost
　　ocean,
Lonely and void, as when the lifeless planet
Moved without eyes to see or ears to hear,

Yet, after uncounted æons,
Out of the clashing of those blind elements,
Endlessly heaving and sinking, tossing their
　　spindrift,
In what still seemed their old unchanging
　　way,
Something—by what wild chemistry?—had
　　arisen;
A vast and terrible Something had—evolved;
Something that had four thousand searching
　　eyes,
And was approaching, through that darkness,
　　now.

[1]

Night still concealed it. Winds and waves
    roared on,
Blind as of old; yet—as that Something
    neared,
The innermost values of the whole dark
    world
Seemed to be changed by its approaching
    power.

Then, with a long-drawn thunder, and blaz-
    ing lights,
A monstrous portent surged across the
    dark. . . .

I saw a great ship, like a lighted City,
Cleaving that night, between two unseen
    worlds.
    .   .   .   .

It passed, and left no trace, and the black
    brine
Heaved, as of old, when the blind lifeless
    planet
Moved without eyes to see, or ears to hear,

THE LAST VOYAGE

Out of this lifeless welter, hither and thither,
Tossing its random spume through endless
    years,
By chance, no more, as the fool's heart or-
    dains,
The life that shaped that monstrous portent
    rose,
Evolved—by what wild miracle? Had the
    less
Brought forth the greater, by those delicate
    grades
And slight divisions wherein the dim-eyed
    sophist
Delights to lose his soul; each grade a gulf
In thought, yet in itself so seeming narrow,
He counts them all as nothing, and leaps the
    abyss
Between the lifeless æons, and this dread
    Now;
When, urged by a purpose, moving to a goal,
That vast arrival thundered through the deep?

Whence? Whither? Why? It passed, and
    left no trace.

And That which lay beyond, the ultimate
    Cause,
And Goal of all—enduring through all
    change—
The self-subsistent, uncontingent, Mover,
What word of That?
              Only the vast black seething;
The salt cold spindrift, and the ghostly surf
As the dark hills dissolved and streamed away
Whispering,—*as it was in the beginning* . . .
Then, challenging, as the great new surges
    rose,
Et nunc, et semper; then that æonian roar
In saecula saeculorum, from beyond
The last horizons of the unsearchable sea.

The mist rolled down; and it was night, black
    night.

I

NIGHT, and the great ship like a lighted city
In mid-Atlantic, cleaving the cold black
    storm;
A city detached from all the coasts of man
Speeding across the abyss of loneliness
Between two unseen worlds.

Unseen, I walked the long deserted decks
That dwindled into the gloom like rain-
    washed streets.
I peered through lighted windows; heard the
    sound
Of music from its wide, bright, pillared
    rooms,
Crowded with festive tables, gay with flowers.

I stole up shining corridors; and saw
In one dim cabin, under shaded lights,
A group of graver faces, hushed and still,
Intently watching a flushed unconscious child.

[5]

It was no dream.   I heard her difficult
    breathing.
I saw the white-capped nurse; the kneeling
    mother,
With drawn and quivering under-lip; the
    father
Standing behind her, silent, with one hand
Laid gently on her shoulder; and the surgeon
Two fingers on the child's wrist as he
    counted . . .
The gleam of the ticking watch.

                               At last he rose,
Muttering to the father—"I shall come back,
In half an hour."

                          Outside the purser's office
The captain met him.

                  "How is your little patient?"
"No hope, unless I operate.   It's a risk.
One chance in a thousand.   If only we could
    have made
New York in time, Johns Hopkins has a man
That might have saved her.   It will be too
    late.

[6]

We're fifteen hundred miles away to-
night."—
"Your skill and your experience. . . ."
                              "Ah, but this
Is different. It's a case for specialists.
A fair all-round musician can't compete
With Kreisler—not in Bach. Besides, at sea,
We haven't half the equipment."—
                        "What is the name
Of this Johns Hopkins' man, who might have
    saved her?"—
—"Marlowe. I wish to God I could consult
    him."—
—"I think you can. He is on his way to
    Europe.
I saw his name in our own wireless news
This morning. He is somewhere on the At-
    lantic."—
—"What ship?"—
            "The *City of Paris.*"—
                        "Where is she now?"
"Four hundred miles away."
                        He beckoned the purser—

"Telephone up to the wireless-room, and tell
them
To get the *City of Paris* . . . an urgent message
Is coming through, at once."

$\cdot$ $\cdot$ $\cdot$ $\cdot$ $\cdot$ $\cdot$ $\cdot$ $\cdot$

The storm roared
And whistled across the bare, dark, upper
deck
As they climbed up to the small bright wire-
less-room.
All round them surged the night of midmost
ocean,
Inhuman, void, as when the lifeless planet
Moved without eye to see, or ear to hear,
Unconscious through the unconscious. . . .
Four hundred miles away, through that black
night,
The *City of Paris,* plunging the opposite way,
Bore, in the midget span of one man's brow
The saving light—a little vanishing spark . . .
Sundered from those who needed it, by gulfs
Of thundering darkness, leagues of volleying
sleet,

THE LAST VOYAGE

Wild howling maelstroms of the world of
    matter,
Through which, outside the wireless-room, no
    voice
Could pierce, no message pass from mind to
    mind.
They closed the padded door. The tumult
    died.

At once, in that small luminous inner realm,
Through deeper regions, undisturbed by
    storm,
Annihilating space the signals came.
Tap-tap, tap-tap, the moving finger wrote.
Five hundred miles to westward the *Majestic*
Told the *Homeric,* far to eastward now,
Of hurricanes approaching. *Tap-tap-tap*
The dark *Leviathan* answered from the north.
The listener, with the head-clips, heard their
    voices
In an ethereal calm. As though a child
Were playing with its toys, three feet away.
The *Mauretania,* surging through the night,

Six hundred miles to southward, droned its
    tale.
Carmania, like an elfin horn, replied
Nearing the fog-bound Banks; while, racing
    home,
Under clear stars, through sleeker softer seas,
The *Berengaria* flung her deeper chords
Of welcome and farewell to half the world.

"You have sent our call out?"
                    "Yes—no answer yet.
Ah, here she comes!" *Tap-tap,* a silver note
Rose high and clear, vibrating like a star,
The *City of Paris.*
                The moving finger wrote,
Dot—dash—dot—dash. "Is Dr. Marlowe
    aboard?"
—"Yes"—
"Tell him that the surgeon of the *Olympic*
Wants his advice . . . an urgent case . . . a
    child."
—"I'll send for him, immediately."
                    "Take down
These details in the meantime, and repeat.

Marlowe will understand. When he has read
    them
Give me his answer, as quickly as you
    can." . . .
*Tap-tap, tap-tap, dot—dash, dot—dash, dot—
    dash.*

.   .   .   .

I walked upon the sheltered deck below
While the swift messages passed. I heard the
    sound
Of music, and the shuffle of dancing feet
In the great ball-room; caught a hundred
    gleams
Of separate lives, each going its own way,
While the one ship took all to the one goal,
(As the one planet bears ten thousand ships,
And the one cosmos binds a myriad worlds . . .
Whence? Whither? Why? . . .
                In the dark-panelled lounge
Wreathed with cigar-smoke, voices quietly
    drawled,
Clubs and *No Trumps.* Cards gleamed and
    glasses tinkled.
There, and there only, in solemn make-believe,

I saw the reign of Chance.

                     In the dark bows,
A strange old fellow-passenger, buried and
    swathed
In travelling coat and muffler; his keen face,
All but the deep magnetic eyes, obscured
Beneath his dark slouch hat,—came up and
    joined me.
"You've heard," he said; and as he spoke,
    my flesh
Tingled as at a voice from other worlds.
"They stop the ship at ten, for half an hour,
While our good surgeon operates on that child.
Marlowe advised it, instantly, by wireless.
He'll be in touch throughout."

                  "You think they'll save her?"
He glanced at me and answered, *They* may
    save her.
But who are *They?*"

II

In a small cabin, lit by a single port-hole,
The poet, rapt and tense, took up his pen. . . .

Whose Mind dictated, or whose Will com-
    pelled
His half-unconscious music? Not his own.

But, while he pondered that deep mystery
Of order and control throughout the world,
And groped for one clear instance, only one
Wherein the Eternal Intellect might be seen
Directly at work, upon material things,
Using them, and conveying them to an end
Directly, as the mind uplifts the hand
To ends beyond the scope of 'natural law'
And secondary causes,
                        a strange light
For one wild moment flashed on him. He
    saw
The Supreme Art, the one world-ruling Will,

Directly at work among material things,
He saw them moved—caught the controlling
    Power
In act, where Science dropt its proud pre-
    cision,
And fell back blindly on an empty name—
Instinct. The swallow, drawn across the seas
Like an unerring needle, to its goal.
Instinct. That elfin nest of twigs and clay
Built by the ignorant instrument—in whose
    hand?
Instinct. The bee, a cluster of blind atoms,
Building its architectural honeycomb
With intellectual gold. And, clearer still,
Beyond the scope of chemistry as far
As the artist's canvas from the palette's chaos,
That intricate pattern on a fritillary's wing;
Wherein each separate atom in each grain
Of colour had been driven to its own place,
Blindly, to form that intellectual scheme
Which men call Beauty. On those wings he
    saw
Not only what the scientist sees, the curves
Evolved for flight, or colours for masquerade;

THE LAST VOYAGE

But something beyond use, beyond the scope
And aim of the blind struggle for mere life,—
A clear-cut pattern, a little heavenly plan,
A little wandering isle of art in nature,
Divine mosaic, exquisitely inlaid
As with celestial jewel-work. "Evolved,
By sex selection," drones the one-eyed sophist.
Do these winged blossoms woo and choose
    their mates, then,
For subtleties of colour and fair design
Beyond the ecstatic sense of half mankind?
Let the world babble. The artist's eye dis-
    cerned
The absolute Master-craftsman in his work,
Work that required no signature.
                    Then, at once,
Translating all into the terms of song,
As though a bird in the unconscious depths
Of his own mind began to sing, he wrote:

    Tell me you
        That sing in the black-thorn
    Out of what Mind
        Your melody springs.

THE TORCH-BEARERS

Is it the World-soul
  Throbs like a fountain
Up thro' the throat
  Of an elf with wings?

Five sweet notes
  In a golden order,
Out of that deep realm
  Quivering through,
Flashed like a phrase
  Of light through darkness.
But *Who* entangled them?
  Tell me, *Who?*

You whose throats
  In the rain-drenched orchard
Peal your joys
  In a cadenced throng;
You whose wild notes,
  Fettered by Beauty,
Move like the stars
  In a rounded song;

Yours is the breath
  But *Whose* is the measure,

THE LAST VOYAGE

Shaped in an ecstasy
  Past all art?
Yours is the spending;
  Whose is the treasure?
Yours is the blood-beat;
  Whose is the heart?

Minstrels all
  That have woven your housen
Of withies and twigs
  With a Mind in-wrought,
Ye are the shuttles;
  But, out of what Darkness
Gather your thoughtless
  Patterns of thought?

Bright eyes glance
  Through your elfin doorways,
Roofed with rushes,
  And lined with moss.
Whose are the voiceless
  Pangs of creation?
Yours is the wild bough:
  Whose is the Cross?

THE TORCH-BEARERS

Carols of light
  From a lovelier kingdom,
Gleams of a music
  On earth unheard,
Scattered like dew
  By the careless wayside,
Pour through the lifted
  Throat of a bird.

III

"The hand that wields the knife
Will be our surgeon's. The controlling mind
Four hundred miles away, through that thick
*   night*
Is whose?" . . .
        The great ship buried her blind bows
In foam.
         "Not Marlowe's! Even his I'd call
Only a subtler instrumental mind,
Through which, as through a thought-
*   exchange, linked up*
With half the world, thousands of other minds
Remote in time, as Marlowe's is remote
In space, are speaking now." . . .

Two voices in the dark, unconsciously
Thus answered my companion. Two dark
    forms
Rug-wrapped in long deck-chairs, behind my
    own,

Talked, while I lingered on the glimmering
    deck
To watch the seamen as they lashed the
    screens
Of flapping, thrashing sail-cloth, all along
The bulwarks on the buffeted weather-side
Against the increasing storm.
                 The first voice, clear
And crisp, was that of the Chief, the astron-
    omer friend
With whom I had watched the stars, one
    summer night
Ten years ago, from Californian hills.
The second up-welled from other and inner
    worlds,
Deep, quiet, musical, as an echo of Dante
In an old mountain-cloister.
                 It revealed
Another friend,—an old Franciscan padre,
Returning home, on his last earthly voyage,
From Rome to Santa Barbara.
                The thoughts
Of all the ship were bent now on one theme—
That child,—her life, or death.

THE LAST VOYAGE

                     I did not turn
To greet those old companions, yet. The spell
Of that strange meeting, like the ghostly
    power
That in old legends, when the planets met
In certain dark conjunctures, gripped the
    world
With sudden meanings, not discerned before,
Constrained me still to listen.
                  Each, as he spoke,
Struck his own chord in the moving
    Symphony,—
"The instrumental mind, in part, is Mar-
    lowe's,"
The first clear voice went on, in wonder and
    awe,
"But all this inter-dependent, intricate web,
The invisible system of ethereal nerves
Connecting mind and hand with waves of will,
Without which both were helpless, whose are
    they?
We learned to use that system, by the help
Of Gilbert, shall we say, whom Verulam
Dismissed with such contempt; Galvani, too,

Ampère and Hertz, Clerk-Maxwell, Hum-
*   phry Davy,*
Faraday, Lodge. Thousands of men, like cells
In one organic brain, have worked together
To make this moment possible, and evoke
That one reply through darkness, to the call
Our ship sent out to-night."

      "And thousands more
To guide our surgeon. Verulam dismissed
Another man, four hundred years ago,
Whose mind, I think, is touching us to-night
With waves of thought, across the abyss of
  Time,
As closely as those others. . . ."

       Time and Space
Died at the word—the rushing waves went
  by
In darkness . . . yet I saw. . . .

IV

Gray's Inn,—a shadowy room, and smoulder-
　　ing there
Like a strange jewel on one high-panelled
　　wall
A dark rich portrait by Sir Anthony More,
English, but all Madrid in colour and line.

　Under it, hunched in a tasselled high-
　　backed chair,
A lean form, with a mean and shifty face
Of empty craft, a green and viperish eye,
And, round his neck, the Chancellor's golden
　　chain.

It was no dream.　The fur on his rich gown
Fluffed grey as he breathed, below the thin-
　　lipped mouth.
He choked a cough.　I heard the golden
　　links

Tinkling against his breast. . . .

                        Facing him sat
A short and thick-set man with shining eyes
Blithe as black cherries, in a thought-
    ploughed face
Of olivaster hue; his raven hair
Already streaked with grey; and, at his side,
For all his cheer, a dagger.

                    "So you think
You've made a great discovery, Doctor
    Harvey,"
The lawyer sneered, "and yet, not only Galen,
But Homer knew the motion of the blood.
There's nothing strange in that. There's not
    a maid
That blushes, when she meets her lover's eye,
But knows your mighty secret, and would pay
A handsome fee to cure it.

                Doctor Harvey,
You should observe more closely. We need
    facts,
Not theories. Now my own philosophy
(Formed, as you know, in such brief hours of
    leisure

THE LAST VOYAGE

As I could borrow from affairs of State,
And therefore couched in very general
    terms)
Shows a new method of approaching Nature,
Through facts alone. It will transform the
    world,
It will pluck down the Stagyrite, and de-
    throne
The pride of Plato. Had you but observed
My rules, and looked to facts; had you but
    seen,
Noted, considered, one poor maiden's blush,
And all that poets from the birth of Time
Have writ of those blood-roses in her face,
You had been spared the very pretty fall
That waits on all such—idols. Doctor
    Harvey,
I have heard already several of your friends
Calling you crack-brained. You will lose
    your clients.
You were a good physician. Rest on that;
But leave philosophy to the master-minds.
Wrens have their nests and eagles have their
    eyry

From which they scan the world."
                                    The little man
Flushed red.
  "I did not mean to boast, Lord Bacon,"
He answered softly, but with glinting eye.
"Nor did I hope to rob you of the fame
Which your philosophy, published from the
    heights
(Of statesmanship and law), must needs com-
    mand.
Hundreds of other men have played their
    part
In what I called my own; and, as you say,
The motion of the blood is nothing new,
Though hitherto it seemed a random flux,
Uncertain as the breeze that fills the sail
Of our Virginian voyagers." At that phrase,
As under Raleigh's eye, the Chancellor
    winced.
"But now," continued Harvey, with a smile,
"A moment comes when all the separate facts
Whereof you speak so truly, may be seen
As notes in one great system. They obey
A single law. The motion of our earth

Was nothing new, but. . . ."

"I reject it wholly,"
The lawyer snapped.

"Your lordship may be right,"
The little doctor answered, "and I bow
To your decision; but when Copernicus. . . ."

"The prince of charlatans," the Chancellor
sneered,
"A Roman priest, a canon of the Church,
Who flouted the plain sense of all mankind,
And troubled even Rome; a fabulist
Without a scruple, who would introduce
His fictions into Nature. Read your Bible.
The Bible says that Joshua stopped the sun;
And though, as I have many a time averred,
Theology and Science cannot clash
(Because they never meet), there are occasions
When eyes confirm the truth that Scripture
tells.
Our eyes can see the movement of the sun.
The judgment of mankind has made our earth
Central and motionless. Therefore I accept
The fact incorporate in our daily speech,—
'Sun-rising' and 'sun-setting.' Sir, my system

Trusts to the senses, and depends on facts."—
   "But Galileo's glass! . . ."
               —"The glass was flawed
Or Galileo lying! I prefer
Our natural eyesight, Harvey."
                    "Yet the lens
That aids our natural sight is natural, too.
I leave the Tuscan to more starry souls;
But this new microscope. . . ."
              "Ah, Harvey, Harvey,
Another idol! How can it ever achieve
All those fantastic promises? What is glass
That it should open all those heights and
    depths
Where eyes have failed. Now, could you
    turn your lens
To a more natural purpose, use its powers
Of concentrating rays to kindle fires;
Or even, as an instrument of war,
Construct a burning-glass of monstrous size
Through which the sun might strike an
    enemy blind,
You'd then be following the true laws of
    thought

Inductively, to their own natural ends.
We need induction, Harvey, based on facts;
But, first, the facts. . . ."

       "And, therefore, first the power
To recognise and group them in their own
Significant order; and this knowledge comes,
Most often, in an unexpected gleam,
Like memory, an intuitive synthesis,
Or a new light from heaven——"

              "We must trust
Our senses, Harvey."

         "And they still deceive us.
The colours of the world are in our eyes;
The music of the world is in our ears;
And only when the microcosmic mind
Of man has made its own swift synthesis,
Does it reflect, in moments of strange light,
Whether in art or science, beauty or truth,
The macrocosmic harmonies of God.
This means, I take it, that the world is made
For souls; and that God's image here on earth
Communes with its Creator, as it reads
The hieroglyphs of this material world;
Though these are only shadows."

              [29]

THE TORCH-BEARERS

"I perceive

You are still a slave of Plato. Give me facts."
  "So be it, then. The blood, that kingly
    river,
Flows through the frame, as Rabelais knew.
    But how?
There is a rhythmic order in its flow
As noble as the movement of the heavens;
More noble; for this little realm of man
Sustains a spirit above all Space and Time.
Galen discovered much. He called the heart
The acropolis of the body. He believed
There were two streams of blood, one bright,
    one dark,
The bright stream flowing thro' the arteries
    only,
The dark stream flowing only thro' the veins.
They did not form one system. Sylvius
    traced
The network of the veins; and Winter found
That air gave up its brightness and its life
For some mysterious purpose in the lungs;
But all these facts were unrelated still.

[30]

THE LAST VOYAGE

They did not form one system. That strange
    gleam
Of recognition; that swift synthesis
Within the mind, which dawns like memory,
Discovering, not a new thing, but an old,
Something that, though unseen, was always
    there—
Had not yet lightened on us."

"Facts, my friend,
"Not these Platonic visions!"
                  "Hear me first.
Vesalius found the valves within the veins,
But did not see their purpose—why they
    locked
Their little purple gates against the stream
In one direction only. Then Servetus
Whom Calvin, the Reformer, burned alive,
Found that the life-stream, flowing through
    the lungs,
Drew its bright crimson from the fresh-
    drawn breath.
He saw no more. But so the moment came
Which, in a single flash, revealed the whole,

The single pulsing microcosmic plan
Which imaged the Creator in His work.
That crowning moment, by the grace of God,
Was mine, though I know well how little
    mine.
I traced the bright arterial stream of blood
To its remotest ends. I saw it flow,
The self-same stream, back thro' the delicate
    veins,
Darkening with wastage, driven by that
    strong tide
Behind it, back to the central throbbing heart,
And thence, once more, into the breathing
    lungs
To draw fresh crimson from the winds of
    heaven
And pour fresh life through all the mortal
    frame:
A steadfast rhythm, beyond our blind control
Sustained, dictated, measured by the Will
Of One above, the Supreme Artifex."
"And your chief clue to this?" . . .
                "The valves that locked
In one direction only. I asked myself

THE LAST VOYAGE

What purpose. . . ."
       "Ah, my friend, you are not the first
To follow that old Jack-o-Lent of the mind.
In my philosophy, now, I wholly abjure
The clue of final causes. I depend
On facts, and facts alone. There was a time
When I was greatly vexed with monstrous
    warts,
Caused, I believe, by handling of a toad
In one of my inquiries; for my hands
Grew like two toads themselves, with warts
    as large
And yellow as cowslip-buds, but cold—like
    stones.
Physicians had no remedy. Moons went by,
And every wart they killed engendered five.
They worked on theories. Then I learned a
    fact
And cured them. How? A lady of the court
Told me of something she had heard in
    France.
She said that if I nailed a lump of fat
Outside my window, as the sun dissolved it
The warts would melt away. I did not ask

[33]

14669

For theories. I was well content with facts—
Facts I could test, observe with my own eyes;
And so I nailed the fat up, in the sun,
And as the sun dissolved it, day by day,
The warts diminished, till, at one same hour,
Both fat and warts completely disappeared.
That's what I call true method, sir! The
    proof?
Experiment! Observation! And Result!
Look at my hand, sir, clean as any babe's.
I spoke of it to Gilbert, whom you know."
   "Good God!" said Harvey, "what did Gil-
    bert say?"—
"He only stared and muttered. He was vexed
Because I rallied him on his false ideas,
His idols, as I call them. He maintains
Some wild magnetic theories, which he thinks
Will one day change the world."
         "Please God, they will,"
Breathed Harvey to himself. "But I suppose
God places these obstructions in our way
To make us fight for victory, and acquire
New strength in fighting."
         "But you never told me—
      [34]

THE LAST VOYAGE

What think you of that other cure I found
For heaviness of the mind. It is well-known
That apes are of a lively disposition;
And I suggested that a young ape's head
New-severed, and applied, sir, like a poultice
Against the nape of the neck, might well
    transmit
Its virtues."

        Harvey smiled. "I have no doubt
Our pharmacists are right when they declare
That torments of the brain may be relieved
By wearing, on the dry, hot, throbbing brow,
Frontlets of roses, wet with morning dew;
Cool water-lilies; acid elder-drupes,
Plucked from the innermost darkness of the
    tree;
A frog's webbed feet; an oyster, stuffed with
    snow;
Moist kernels of ripe peaches; or (an aid
Which I prefer, and they omit, sometimes)
A very simple strip of linen, dipt
In cold spring-water. . . ."

        The Lord Chancellor's eyes
Revolved portentously. "My chief complaint

Against the state of learning in this age
Is its defective reasoning. Your reply
Well illustrates its vagueness. I contend
That unguents are absorbed, virtues inhaled,
And poisons, too, as every murderer knows,
By subtle transpirations through the skin.
There's nothing cures a bout of sleeplessness
Like yolks of egg and powdered poppy-seed,
Not eaten, sir, but poulticed on the skin,
And many an inward torment is appeased
By plastering the intestines of a wolf,
Warm and new-killed, against the naked
    belly;
The sufferer's body, meanwhile, being
    wrapped
In bloody wolf-skins. Why? It is well
    known
That wolves are beasts of great edacity,
And my new method, by induction leads
Clearly to this conclusion—that their guts
Must comfort weaker bowels."

                "Oh, my God,"
Groaned Harvey, under breath.

                "Not only this,"

Continued the great lawyer. ".I contend
That, as these vital influences may pass
Inward, so, also, if we take no care,
We may exhale our spirits through the skin,
And thereby hasten death. Now, my new
    method,
(Which needs no special gift, for all can use
    it)
Leads to this clear conclusion. We should
    coat
Our bodies, close their pores up, with a wax
Which would prevent our sweating life away
So lavishly in summer. . . ."

                 "God have mercy,"
Groaned Harvey, once again; and, as he
    groaned,
The lawyer, waxing eloquent, proclaimed
Not his own thoughts, but something that he
    grasped
Only in general terms, a spirit breathed
Into the common air by greater men
Whom he rejected.

            " 'Tis for us to build
Science anew, by a far nobler method.

[37]

Plato is dead, and Aristotle dust.
We shall observe and test and climb to truth
And. . . ."
    As the soul revolts against the sound
Of God's own praises from a vacuous mind,
The little doctor's gorge began to rise
Against this Pharisee of the Intellect,
Whose very *New Atlantis* was a theft
Marred in the stealing, from Sir Thomas
    More;
And all that he could hear was *quack, quack,*
    quack;
And *quack, quack, quack,* and *quack, quack,*
    quack again.
At last the Chancellor paused. His eye grew
    crafty
His voice dropt.
    "You have had distinguished patients,
Concerning whose infirmities you must know
More than their nearest friends. Indeed, you
    hold
Such knowledge as might help me greatly now
In certain state affairs. If I but knew . . ."

He whispered something that made Harvey
    shrink
And stare at him.
              The little doctor rose.
The things that had been whispered, then,
    were true.
This was a man that could destroy his friend,
And Raleigh's ghost was glimmering at his
    side.
  "Nay, Harvey! State-craft goes with sci-
    ence here.
'Tis nothing more than science—to employ
Our knowledge of the elements in a man—
The chemistry of life. It is no time
For squeamishness. Men of the world must
    take
The world at its own value."
              Harvey bowed
With irony in his heart.
              "So much depends
Upon our choice of worlds, then," he re-
    plied.
"Your lordship will forgive me if I say
That, in *my* world, there is a pagan code,

[39]

A pagan oath . . ."

    "Hippocrates is dead,"
The Chancellor interrupted.

      "Not so dead,"
Said Harvey, "as a hundred I could name
Who still offend the sun. His words endure.
They have been quietly handed down through
  time
By all his followers; and that pagan code,
That pagan oath, though every other fail,
Thank God, his poor benighted followers
  keep."
—"I have heard of it, of course," the Chan-
  cellor smiled,
"But never saw the text . . ."

     "The terms are quaint.
They take for granted old out-worn ideas,
Curious conventions, airy absolutes,
(Honour, for instance) which inductive
  thought
Divorced from—Plato's method (shall we
  say?)
Or wed to Machiavelli, would ignore.

THE LAST VOYAGE

But, roughly, they run thus.   (You will for-
    give
The crude fantastic rhetoric of the dead):

I swear by Paian Apollo, the Physician;
By Æsculapius and his radiant daughters,
(Health and All-heal) Hygieia, Panakeia,
And all the gods and goddesses in heaven,
That I will keep this oath:
To look on him who taught me this great art
As my own father and, in after years,
If need should rise, to share my substance with
    him;
To look upon his sons as my own brothers,
And, if they should desire it, freely impart
My knowledge to them, asking for no
    guerdon;
To hand this light of knowledge on, un-
    dimmed,
To my own sons, and every true disciple
Who takes the self-same oath, but to none
    other;
To pass my life, and practise this great art
In righteousness; that, whatsoever house

[41]

I enter, I bring help to all that need,
And work no evil or corruption there;
That whatsoever I may hear or see,
In entering thus the hidden lives of men,
Shall still be locked in silence.
                While I keep
This oath inviolate, may I still enjoy
The practice of this art, honoured by all,
In every age and clime; but, if I break it,
Then may I be dishonoured."
              The Chancellor smiled
In silence, for ten seconds. Then he sneered,
"As you remarked, this rhetoric of the dead
Has a fantastic sound. Well—Doctor
   Harvey,
You will remember that a word from me
About your—great achievement, would re-
   sound
Through Europe; but I shall not speak that
   word.
You will remain—a wren.
              But this, of course
Will make it no less dangerous for yourself
To indulge in petty jealousies, or hints

THE LAST VOYAGE

That I have any reason to condemn
Your theories, but my preference for facts."
His narrowing eyes
Flashed, suddenly, like a viper's, as he rose,
And Harvey caught that gleam.

                         "I well believe,"
He answered, slowly, like a man too dense
To grasp the deadly meaning, and thereby
Baffling his foe with doubt, "I well believe
That all your lordship's curious—facts, will weigh
More potently than mine, in after days.
They are vouched for by the Lord High Chancellor,
Who can impose his greatness on the world
With all the awe attached to his high place.
Therefore, in future ages, when the world
Discovers other—facts, and no more reads
Or cares for what we say, your lordship's fame,
Spread by your lordship's eloquence, will content
The world that hears it echoing, and must take
(In general terms and principles, at least)

Greatness like yours on trust.

> But I must go.

I have a tryst with Science."

> He groped out,

Into that dark, that blind, that crooked street,
Called by the crowd *Obscurity,* to join
Gilbert, of whose blind idols half the laws
That rule the new electric world were
> born. . . .

V

Night, on the loud Atlantic, boundless night;
Electric messages, flashing, through the storm
Like broken gleams of an order whereof
    man's thought
Had only discovered a fragment; and, under
    it all,
One voice, *You think they will save her!*
    Swift! Be swift!
Or knowledge will come too late!
                  As when the mind
Strives with the paralysed body, and strives
    in vain
To flash the imperative will through the
    leaden limbs
And rule once more, the single organic whole;
Or as the first strange nervous currents that
    thrill
The slow developing embryo, ere it grows
Into co-ordinate unity and power;

[45]

So now, thro' the boundless night of Space
    and Time,
From the centres of thought, and the brain-
    cells of the world,
From the Æsculapian springs on the ancient
    heights,
From the vine-clad islands of Cos in the Myr-
    toan sea,
Where Burinna, the fount of Hippocrates,
    murmurs and flows,
And the tree of Hippocrates bends with the
    weight of its years;
From the centres of light and remembrance,
    Athens and Rome,
Salerno, Bologna, and Paris; from rose-col-
    oured towers
Of Heidelberg, throned o'er the Necker, but
    gazing afar
On the air-blue castles and mist-wreathed
    crags of the Rhine;
From Padua, *alma mater* of Harvey's dreams,
Where the shadow of good Fabricius walks
    and talks
With the shadow of Galileo, all night long;

[46]

THE LAST VOYAGE

From the new electric cities of power and
speed,
London, Berlin, and the towers of the western
world;
The militant intellect flashed its messages out,
Struck thro' the dense blind bulk of things
and strove
To make of our chaos that interdependent
whole
Which the mind and the spirit could use for
each and all,
Each being the centre of all, as that ship in
the night,
And the child on the ship, were the centre of
heaven's wide dome,
Wherever the child and the ship and the
planet might move.
Ten thousand minds, with that one small life
at stake,
Unconsciously laboured there, each set on its
task,
And each set apart, with its own small lamp
in the dark,

[47]

In its own strict bounds, the better to serve
    the whole.
But always, at every blunder, and each delay,
I heard that terrible whisper—*Swift! Be
    swift,*
Or knowledge will come too late.
You think they will save her?
Delayed by folly, baffled and beaten again
By lethargy, in man's own sleep-walking
    world,
Driven back in defeat by the nightmare chaos
    of war
But finding new light, even there, on that
    blood-red road;
The struggle went on; each age with a broken
    cry
Ars longa, vita brevis, re-echoing still
The cry of Hippocrates, Galen and Harvey in
    turn,
But flinging the deathless fire with a dying
    hand
To youth that should follow and conquer. . . .
              Swift! Be swift!

THE LAST VOYAGE

Burn thro' all obstacles now with the lightning
    of law.
Seize the swift fire, or the knowledge will
    come too late!
What years they were wasting on speed to an
    alien goal,
Or ever Boerhaave, and Hunter and Lister
    were born,
While the tardy discoverer dallied with
    dreams that should grow
To ripeness, only through centuries, after what
    pain;
Or the thinker crouched in a ditch, while the
    chaos of battle
Shattered and trampled his life's work into
    the mire.

VI

Edgehill, red sun on stubble, steel blades in
    the sun;
Rupert, a-flash in the saddle, and galloping by
At the head of his thundering mail-clad
    cavalry charge
Plumed, mailed, with face up-lifted, as if to
    sing;
Shouts of command; quick flickering tongues
    of fire;
The blind concussion of guns in the welter of
    smoke
That swallowed the cavalry, only a furlong
    away;
Death in the air!
       And Harvey, the King's physician,
Crouching under a hedge, in a sheltering
    ditch,
Where innocent wild-flowers, blind to the
    madness of men,
Smiled at the sun.

THE LAST VOYAGE

      The two young princes were there,
Crouching beside him. . . . He rubbed a red
    stain from his hand
With a dark green dock-leaf. . . .
           "No," he was saying, "you twist
The tourniquet tight, round the limb, on the
    side of the wound
Farthest away from the heart, if it's blood
    flowing back
Thro' the veins; but if it comes pulsing, jetting
    and bright
From an artery, fasten your tourniquet
    quickly above,
Between the wound and the heart."
           He plucked a great poppy,
Pressed its dark core to his nostrils, and
    quickly breathed,
"Could we only discover an opiate, something
    to drown
The pangs of the body in sleep, while we work
    with the knife,
What thousands on thousands of lives would
    be saved.

Poor Scrope
Had twenty-four terrible gashes. To those
who explore
The marvels of this most delicate house of the
soul,
This human body, the Temple of God upon
earth,
What sacrilege thus to misuse it!"
Then, raising his voice,
He spoke to the listening princes,

"Did Galen not say
That his work on the Use of the Body was
naught but a hymn
To the God and Creator of all. *Conditori,*
he wrote,
Verum hymnum compono—

For Galen, the truest of prayers
Was the search for the truth, the striving to
know, and make known,
The wisdom, the power, and the infinite goodness of God.
We grieve when we look on an exquisite tap-
estry torn,

THE LAST VOYAGE

A picture disfigured, a Parian masterpiece
    wrecked,
A desecrate shrine; yet—yet—with our wars
    and our sins
What havoc we make of God's image. . . ."
He shook his white head. He drew from his
    pocket a book.
"God help, and forgive us," he muttered.
    "Come—let us forget
These horrors awhile. Don't look at their hell
    any more.
I'll read to you till I am needed. We'll try
    to shut out
Their chaos; lay hold on the cosmos that
    underlies all,
The cosmos of music. . . .
You know those great lines of the *Georgics*
Happy is he who can search out the causes
    of things,
For thereby he masters all fear, and is throned
    above fate.
The Latin says less; but my rendering, read
    by the light

[53]

Of those other great lines in his Æneid, can
   hardly be wrong:

Are not the sky and the earth, and the wild-
   flowing plains of the ocean,
Ay, and the moon on her way, and the sun in
   his chariot of splendour,
All sustained from within, by a Spirit, a Mind
   in the cosmos,
Moving the blindfold mass. . . .
Et magno se corpore miscet. . . ."

Was it thunder of horsemen, or only the rush
   of the waves?
Was it only the pulse of the turbines, down in
   the dark?
The throb of mechanical pistons, obeying a
   law,
Moving in rhythm, but shaped and controlled
   by a Mind;
But used for a purpose, and aimed at what unseen goal?

VII

The lamps gleamed out along the well-
  screened decks.
The wind keened through the cordage, and I
  heard
The Atlantic seething by. . . .
                                    Was I awake
In that far world, or was I dreaming now?
Two rug-wrapped forms behind me, in deck-
  chairs
Were talking of that child—and that strange
  fight
With Time and Space to save her.
                        "What does it mean,—
This intricate organisation of the world
Into a single interdependent whole?"
The Chief was speaking, my astronomer
  friend.
"What does it mean? This growth of our
  control
Over our space-time world, the racing ships,

[55]

The electric word, and more mysterious far,
That inconceivable speed of cosmic light
Which is controlled by Something, not our-
    selves,
Controlled and urged in endless rhythmic
    waves,
Flashing for ever through the unplumbed
    abyss
For some inscrutable end, from star to star.
What *can* it mean?   An urgency so vast.
And so stupendous, flashing on and on,
Through endless ages, with such constancy,
And such perfection of organic law
That we forget its movement and its power,
An urgency that links all worlds in one
(For what deep purpose and at whose com-
    mand?)
Must have an aim stupendous as itself,
In God's own counsels.

Padre, there are times—"
His voice dropped low, and deepened with his
    thought—
"When, on my lonely mountain-top, the sense

THE LAST VOYAGE

Of this appalling mystery drives my thoughts
To the sheer brink of madness. I look up
And out, beyond our Milky Way, and see
Those twisting nebulæ, like coils of mist
Where suns as vast as our whole universe
Are less than atoms. Then, beneath my feet
I see the dust, of which each molecule now,
Rends open, in its infinitesimal heart,
Unfathomable gulfs of suns and stars.
And man, who sails midway between the
     heights
And depths, and is the measure of them all,
Can only dream that, as his own control
Of Nature grows with his own growing mind,
So the Supreme Control, from depth to height,
Of all this moving universe abides
With the one Perfect Will and Supreme
     Mind."

Then, in the dark, the second voice replied,
"That's what we seek for, in our mortal blind-
     ness,—
The deep-set unseen Centre that controls
The vast organic cosmos it evolves

Through Time and Space.   Armies of facts
    are ours.
They crowd upon us till our knowledge melts
Into a wilder chaos.   Ant-like men,
As that lost poet said, go staggering by
Balancing awful libraries of fact
On their bald skulls, while, more than all, we
    need
Co-ordinating power to grasp and use
The knowledge we have gained.   We need a
    mind
To grasp your own discoveries as one whole
With ours, who, also, in our age-long war,
Experience and observe some flaming truths;
So that our future Faradays need not say
'I enter another room, and lock my doors
On science, when I kneel.'   With such a mind,
We might achieve, not that armed truce of
    thought
Between the Faith and Science, reconciled
Only to pass, and shun each other's gaze,
But that great golden symphony of thought
Which, long ago, the Angelic Doctor heard
Throbbing from hell to heaven, organic truth,

THE LAST VOYAGE

Wherein each note, in its own grade, rings
    clear,
As in a single orchestra, whose chords
Were chaos, till each filled its own true place
In the one golden cosmos of the song.
We should discover, then, that all the gulfs
Between your friends and mine, are gulfs in-
    deed,
But only gulfs, not clashing contraries.
We need a new Aquinas now to bridge them,
A pontifex to make our sundered truths
As true a whole as, in each human frame,
The orchestral personality of man,
That microcosm, clothed with mortal clay,
Quickened by all the accordant senses,
    crowned
By thought; and subtly ennobled, lifted
    higher,
By that strange power which, in our darkness
    kneels,
And sometimes moves the world. For man
    himself,
In his mysterious unity, images
The hierarchic cosmos, through all grades

THE TORCH-BEARERS

From earth's blind clay, up to the supreme
    Mind
Which moves and rules the whole. The
    separate note
Not only plays its part within that Whole,
But is itself a symphony in little;
An atom, filled with music, by the wheels
Of planetary electrons, which reflect
The music of the spheres.

                    All analogues
Fail; but we need that deeper monist now,—
Not one who delves only to find the skull
Skin-deep beneath the skin, and everywhere
Under the surface finds new surfaces;
But one who reads, in Nature's crookéd script,
Scrawled on the rocks or scrolled within the
    sky,
The eternal hieroglyphs; and truly sees
As Plato, for one burning moment, saw,
Through earth's distorting shadows, Beauty
    enthroned;
Or as that strange Emanuel of the Moon,
The wild philosopher-fabulist, Swedenborg,
Mightiest of all the minds that ever crashed

THE LAST VOYAGE

To madness in the splendour of that Gaze
Which none can meet and live, still lived to
    see
The secret correspondences of earth
And all its laws with that celestial world;
Walked through all gardens as thro' Paradise,
And talked with angels on his native hills
As on the hills of heaven.
                  Science now
So strangely nears by its own arduous road
The idealist's world. . . . Your atomists have
    dissolved
Their old material 'solids' into a mist
Not so unlike the veil that Berkeley drew
Between his face and God.
                That thin bright mist
Of protons and electrons veils a power
That might annul or neutralise them all,
So that, like Prospero's gorgeous pageantry
This universe of dense material forms
Might, in the apostle's 'twinkling of an eye,'
Melt into spirit-realms, where we should see
As when the film of cataract is removed
From blinded eyes, and all the coloured fields

Shine out anew, with flocks on distant hills;
Or when that veil which hides the ethereal
  world
Was rifted, and men heard behind the storms
Of their own world, in deep unbroken calm
Those radiant messages, calling and replying,
Across the Atlantic night. If our poor toys,
Our webs of wire, hung in the whistling wind,
Give us these glimpses of unguessed at realms,
What splendour and what music, what full
  blaze
Of vivid life may burst on us, when Death
Strips off the cataract-veils of this dull flesh.
The analogue fails, yet this discovery, too,
This wireless miracle, like a lightning flash,
Confirms old gropings into the dark beyond;
Brings us a little nearer, not to heaven,
But to a glimpse, by parable, if you will,
Of how some ancient thoughts which men cast
  off
As idle tales, came nearer to the truth
Than their first thinkers knew;
Suggests analogous laws in deeper realms,

THE LAST VOYAGE

Hints at the means whereby Omniscience
  works,
When prayer strikes home to the deep heart
  of things.
Did not the Angelic Scholar who unfolded
Out of the Aristotelian acorn all
Those heaven-embracing boughs for Dante,
  write,—
Immortal spirits, transcending Space and
  Time
Can instantly be present where they will;
Even as their thought, without process of
  reason,
Grasps in immediate vision, all that man,
By slow discourse, groping from point to
  point,
Sees but in fragments, losing what he won
On other heights, when he attains to new.
For seldom, even in memory, man holds fast
The splendours he saw clearly yesterday;
Nor, though the Way inexorably leads him
On to new splendours, does the new atone
For all he leaves behind, till on the last
Consummate height, full memory returns

With the full vision; and, in the mind of God,
He sees the eternal aspect of the whole.
There, as Augustine says, the glorified body
Moves wherever it will, to every distance,
Like the sun's ray; for, in the City of God,
Wherever the spirit listeth, it shall be.
There shall we run, and not be weary again;
Because the world is conquered. There the
    mind
Using the bridle of law constrains and guides
Dumb Nature, as in ancient days, the Power
Rode into Jerusalem, on a foal that wore
A cross upon its shoulders. Here the palms
Of victory are soon withered; but, in heaven,
Our warfare is accomplished. Here, on earth,
The mind of man is like a little mirror,
Reflecting what it faces, and no more.
Carry it up the intellectual heights
And it will show you parables, one by one,
In crag and pine and cloud. The wayside
    flower
Will float within it, and the mountain eagle
Gyre through its midget sky. It will reveal
A dark earth-cleaving valley, a snowy peak,

THE LAST VOYAGE

Up-towering; each a fragment, a bright patch
Of colour, a delicate shadow, a broken image
Of that Completeness which must still escape
    it.
For, round each gleaming picture, the blind
    frame
Of man's own mind shuts out the Whence and
    Why.
Letters and words we read, not sentences
Of the world's volume . . . single hiero-
    glyphs,
Not the vast epic of the eternal hills
Like armies of archangels thundering home
Into the mind of God.
                We stare through heaven
And see a moment's eddy, a flying whirlpool
On that dark river of stars;
But all its intricate intellectual systems,
Wheeling around the one eternal Throne,
Are hidden more deeply from man's plodding
    reason,
Escape the range of that small mirror's eye,
More utterly than the towers of the New
    World,

Evade the mind and eye of a nestling wren
Under its mother's breast, in a creviced wall,
Among the coombs of Devon.   Yet this glory
Is ours, and not the wren's, that we discern
Our failure, which is victory, in the end.
For, by the measurement of our loss we know
Something of what we lose.   That deep abyss,
An infinite vacuum, opening in our minds
To earth's and heaven's abhorrence must be
    filled.
Like rushing air, like a wild ocean plunging
Over a precipice, the whole universe,
And all that it can give, wealth, knowledge,
    power,
May then be drawn into that infinite void;
But it is never filled till God Himself
Flow into it, with His Love, which is our
    peace."

VIII

In her dim cabin, above the unconscious child,
The mother bowed her head,
Remembering, not repeating with her lips,
The old supplication to the God in Man. . . .
I am not worthy, Lord, that Thou shouldst
  enter
Under my roof. Thy word, Lord, from
  afar. . . .
I cannot understand the terrible powers
Encompassing us—only that they confirm
Thy power, and all their laws are but Thy
  will.
I cannot pray 'Thy will, not mine, be done';
Not now; not now. At every other time,
But oh, not now. Save me but this, dear Lord.
Mine is the prayer from which Thy soul re-
  frained,
In Thine own agony, to the Eternal Father,
Who could have sent Thee, instantly, from
  Heaven,

THE TORCH-BEARERS

Legions of angels. As the words of man
Have struck across the darkness and the storm,
Stand Thou far off, but send Thy healing
*   word.*

IX

I passed the door of the operating-room.

Two white-capped nurses with their cool
    quick hands
Had stripped a spacious cabin, and laid out
A bare clean table.
                All was ready now.
The clinging pungent breath of the antiseptic
Crept through the long white corridor and
    submerged
Its oily smells of rubber and heated paint. . . .

"God, but it carries you back," a voice said,
    passing.
"Whiffs of iodoform, blowing all over France,
From every village behind the lines. It killed
Even the smell of the gasoline. . . ."
                Then those two,
Walking behind me again, voicing my
    thoughts,

Like voices heard in a dream.

"Not long ago,
They only laughed when Lister. . . ."

"He has joined
Those other voices now, beyond the storm.
How many lives has Lister saved since then?"

"In eighteen-seventy, armies rotted to death
For lack of what he taught us; and the knife
Sent more than half its victims to the grave.
So Lister, whom they sneered at, must have
   saved
Some fifty million lives throughout the world,
Men, women, children."—

"More than thrice the number
That fifteen nations, slaughtering night and
   day,
For those five years of glorious war. . . ."

"And now
Here, in the ship, that child would die to-
   night,
Had it not been for Lister."

"But the mind
That flashed the light on Lister?"

[70]

THE LAST VOYAGE

                              "As I said
'*They* still may save the child.   But who are
    They?' "

With that strange question echoing in my
    brain
I reached my cabin, and shut all voices out,
All but the swish of the long wave rushing by.
Then, as I lay in the dark, with eyes half
    shut,
One broken glimpse, as though an angel tried
To answer a child's question with a picture
Shown in a magic mirror, one fleeting glimpse
Of all that intricate interdependent whole
Gleamed on me, and I saw,—
I saw, as if thro' a port-hole opening there
Its gleaming round in the solid and brass-
    bound walls
Of our space-time world, a magical vision,
    alive
As the living truth,—an exquisite old French
    village,
Embosomed in vine-clad hills.

It was no dream.
The bird's nest cottages, washed with lilac and
rose,
The brown thatched roofs, with flowers grow-
ing out of the thatch,
Each side of the bright little straggling sun-
bathed street,
The chuckled delight of the river that flowed
beside them,
Belying its name, *La Furieuse,* dark and
cool;
The delight of the riverside willows, in gleams
of the wind,
Ruffling from green to grey, each leaf as it
turned
Distinct as a sparkle of dew; the clang of the
bell
At the Ursuline convent; the cluck of the hens
at the doors;
The faint sour whiff of the tannery—its brown
yard
So soft underfoot with the tatters of rusty
bark

THE LAST VOYAGE

That carts which had rattled like musketry
    over the cobbles
Out in the street, and the clattering sabots
    beside them
All seemed soundless as dreams as they passed
    its gate;
And, drowning its acrid tang, all round it
    breathed
Lavender, jessamine, roses, in clustering gar-
    dens;
And, clear as in crystal, a little above and
    beyond,
I saw the bright stalls and the butterfly
    splashes of colour
Where seven old witches, with shawls round
    their wicked old shoulders,
Hunched up on the stones of the market-place
    (once a church)
Now turned out their butter, in round pats
    yellow as cowslips,
Now piled up their baskets of onions and rosy-
    cheeked apples,
Now counted their eggs and their money, or
    knitted and chattered.

THE TORCH-BEARERS

It was no dream.
The glint of the sun on their needles;
The chime of a distant forge; the laugh of a
    child;
Cocks crowing and oxen lowing;
All told me this.

Far off, on the deck of a ship, like a voice in
    a dream,
Echoed those words, once more—"You think
    they will save her?"
Far off, in the thick of the dark Atlantic storm
Like a voice in a dream replying,—
They *may save her;*
But who are They?

       And then, as to men in an airship
That swoops to its goal, the heart of their
    vision draws nearer,
One cottage, one garden, grew large in the
    magical window;
And, under a gnarled old mulberry tree, I saw
In a stained blue nankeen blouse, with his
    bare brown legs

THE LAST VOYAGE

Out-straddled in front of an easel, an urchin
    of twelve,
(What fount of our hope was this?) whom
    the town of Arbois,
Had nicknamed 'Louis the Artist.'
                  Look—look long,
Would you fathom those grey-green eyes. . . .
For there, unknown to the world, was the light
    that we looked for,
The fount of our hope for the child on the
    storm-tossed ship,
Far off, in Space and Time, but conquering
    both
As the message that flowed through the ether
    under the storm,
Distinct to the sight, as that other was clear
    to the hearing,
He stood there, making his picture,—
Louis Pasteur.

His bare brown legs apart, his sun-burnt toes
Down-settling into the turf, his mind intent,
He was drawing a neighbour's portrait, in col-
    oured chalks.

THE TORCH-BEARERS

He hummed to himself as he worked,
An odd little ditty, that went to a tune of his
own:

I saw an elf
  Proudly enthroned on a dandelion flower
And singing to himself:

A bee-sized boy
  With little green eyes like emerald
    sparks,
And little red lips of joy!

What sing you there?
  I whispered him soft as a cloud might
    whisper
High up in the April air.

But he sang on
  With less than the heed that a man might
    pay
To a voice beyond the sun.

THE LAST VOYAGE

His sitter, at ease in a chair, with a glass be-
  side him,
Brimmed with red wine, was the Mayor of
  Arbois himself,
Monsieur Pereau,—a little uneasy, perhaps,
Not sure that it wholly befitted his dignity
  thus
To sit for an urchin, and yet, as the lad's
  pastels
Had won such approval (and cost very little).
  Ah, well,
He was there, in his very best uniform,
  braided with silver,
The cross of the Legion of Honour, the tri-
  colour scarf,
And a snowy-white stock, over which his self-
  satisfied face
Smiled rosily down on the sun-burnt artist of
  twelve
Through whom, and through this one hour,
  could the great man know it,
All ages to come might borrow this one swift
  glimpse

Of his plump and benignant memory, other-
 wise lost
In the vast and gloomy abysses that Nature
 reserves
For the special oblivion of mayors.
                        Thus let him emerge
Blue-eyed, from a background of blue, with
 his bristling hair
And the heavy moustache that seemed made
 to be dipped in a froth
Of golden refreshment, and afterwards wiped
 with a napkin.

"Who taught you to draw, mon petit?"
"My father.   He made me this easel."
                    "But tanners don't draw."
"He painted a picture at Marnoy, before we
 came here
On one of the doors of our house.   It shows an
 old soldier,
Tilling the ground like a peasant.   He leans
 on his spade,
In his faded and tattered old uniform, daubed
 with the clay,

And dreams of the Emperor's eagles, against
    a grey sky
And misty blue hills. He painted his memo-
    ries there.
You know that my father was one of the
    Emperor's men,
Though he never will talk of it now——"
                "I know. I have seen him,
On Sundays, he looks very smart, and he wears
    his frock-coat
Like a veteran, too, and his ribbon, the Legion
    of Honour,
Says everything. Why should he speak? I
    myself should be proud
To be one of Napoleon's corporals——"
                "No. It's not pride.
His peasant is bowed, in deep thought. I have
    seen the same look
In his eyes; and one evening, in winter, be-
    side our own fire,
He told me—some things he remembered."
                "Ah, wonderful tales!
The trumpets! The banners!"
    "No! No! They were terrible things!

The thousands and thousands that died in the
    hands of the surgeon,
For lack of——"
           "For lack of——?"
           "I don't understand; but he said
Their wounds had all festered. He thought
    that they needn't have died,
If only——"
           "If only?"
  "Ah well, you would smile if I told you:
For all he could say was just this—if the
    surgeon's own knives,
Before they were used, had been dropt into
    scalding hot water
The chances were better. It happened, by
    accident, once;
And the surgeon scalded his hands, in pulling
    them out;
But after the amputation, although it was bad,
The wound healed best of them all."
              "What reasoning, child!
What nonsense! Boiling the knives!"
           "I knew you would smile.
But—my father—he notices things.

He says that no gardener ever despises a seed
No matter how small it may be.
      He says that the silk-looms of France
Would be idle to-morrow if silkworms forgot
    to lay eggs.
Then half of her riches would go."
                  "Tra la! What a child!
But it's true. Very true. For the women, all
    over the world,
Sail under the fluttering colours of Lyons to-
    day.
They must tread in the sheen of the peacock,
    and shimmer like brooks
When the kingfisher streaks them with blue,
    and the dragon-flies flash.
They must dance in a mist of the sunset, with
    stars in their hair,
And a film of the rainbow to wrap round
    their shoulders at dawn.
My daughters! Tut! tut! But no matter. I
    suffer for France.
The world must have silks."
"And the silkworm its mulberry leaves."

[81]

THE TORCH-BEARERS

They were whispering over his head.
The low wind shivered and breathed through
*   the mulberry leaves,*
Above him, as though it were trying to
*   whisper a thought.*

For the Spirit of Time was there
And it knew that the silk-looms of France
Would be stilled in a few more years
By something that shrivelled the wings
Of the moth in its golden cocoon;
And then, under mulberry boughs,
The boy would be poring, intent,
Through a lens, to discover the cause
In that infinitesimal life
Which swarms in the blood of a gnat
And can bring down a kingdom to death.

And, when he discovered that cause,
And declared that the cause should be crushed,
At once, in the hour of his triumph,
The hate of the world would begin.
Since the cause could only be crushed
By a sacrifice, moments of loss,

[82]

THE LAST VOYAGE

For a gain too great to be told,
The blind brute crowd that he saved
Would pelt him with stones in the streets·
And his envious rivals would turn
And jeer with the ignorant crowd.
In the name of the science he loved,
In the name of the truth he adored,
In the hour when he glorified France
With a splendour that never can die,
When he stretched out his hands to her, filled
With miraculous gifts from his mind,
When he poured out his treasures of thought
At her feet, they would spit in his face,
They would brand him as liar and fool,
And when they had broken his heart,
And basest and bitterest of all,
Robbed him of joy in his task,
They would bid him work on, in the night.
Paralysed, desolate, old. . . .
Not caring at all any more. . . .
And *then*—they would crown him with fame.

For the way of it never has changed,
Though the name of the way will be new

THE TORCH-BEARERS

As each generation arrives,
And discards, not the wrong, but its name.

Yet, paralysed, desolate, old,
He would fight, and fight on till the end;
To the saving, not only of France,
Thro' her silk-looms which, after the War,
Would pay off the Prussian again;
But—on—on—on—thro' the dark
To the saving of myriads of men,
For the light that enkindled his mind
Would be flashed overseas to the North;
Where Lister, the Chief, in the wards
Of that hospital, wrestled with Death
As Heracles wrestled of old.

And on—on—on—through the dark
Of that infinitesimal world
To the proof that no life without life
Could be born, and the infinite goal.

"But it runs back farther than that,"
                              the lad went on,
As though he heard nothing at all.

[84]

THE LAST VOYAGE

        "There's a curious rhyme
He'd repeat to us, saying it showed by what
    fairy-like threads
Past, present and future, are bound in the web
    of the world."

Then the barefoot artist, choosing his creami-
    est chalk
For the plump white hand that reposed on
    the breast of the Mayor,
Lowered his voice and quietly murmured that
    song. . .. .
Was it crooned by himself? Or droned
    through the lavender clump
By a wandering bee, from a garden of mem-
    ory lost
In the drowsy recesses and dim beginnings of
    time?

A princess lived in China
  Two thousand years ago,
And, in her secret garden,
  Great mulberries used to grow

With crooked boughs and spreading leaves
And deep dark roots below. . . .

He broke off, with a smile.

                         "Our fairy-tale
Runs farther back than that. The song means
    nothing
Unless you've heard the tale."

                         "But tell me, then."
"Not I, m'sieu. There is no voice but one
Can tell that tale; and, even so, your ears
Must be attuned to it. If you lie awake
At midnight, you may hear it, in the sound
Of flowing water, or—leaves in a low
    wind. . . ."

And there—as though my half-shut eyes had
    closed
In bodily sleep, but left my soul awake,
The world grew dark; and, in the dark, I
    heard
His voice die out. . . .

                 As when the listener turns
The wireless disk; and, in a single breath,

THE LAST VOYAGE

Moves thro' a continent, hears the murmuring
    throngs
Of capital after capital growing loud
And dying, with guttural scraps of Northern
    speech,
Or softer tones from Mediterranean shores;
A statesman bawling lies; a volley of cheers;
Casino tunes; the shuffle of dancing feet
In far Vienna; or Kreisler's violin
Crying across the Babylonian night;

Or even, in Morse, like faint bewildered
    horns,
Groping through fog, calls of a ship at
    sea. . . .

So, not through Space, but out of the depths
    of Time
A stream of music, softer than the wind
Whispering among the mulberry leaves began
To breathe the tale that Louis refused to
    tell. . . .
A smooth dark stream of rhythm, through
    which I heard

[87]

THE TORCH-BEARERS

Voices that died four thousand years ago
And voices yet unborn, orchestral cries
Of prophecy, and dramatic undertones
Deepening the legend, colouring it with
    thoughts
Beyond the boy's horizon. It seemed to flow
Like that mysterious timeless river of Time
Out of the future, back into the past,
To that strange point where past and future
    meet,
In one eternal and consummate Now.
For, as it whispered through the mulberry
    trees,
It linked the day unborn—when young
    Pasteur
Should seek and find among their rustling
    leaves
The invisible and innumerable hosts
Of death, in worlds of infinitesimal life—
With that lost day, four thousand years ago,
When, to the same low rustling tune, they
    breathed
Through one wild fable, hints of the full
    plan:

THE LAST VOYAGE

Four thousand years ago, in old Pekin,
A queen reigned in a palace, whose wild
    domes
Gleamed like the magic bubbles blown at
    dawn
From ivory hookahs by the dream-drugged
    gods,

Four thousand years ago, in her lost garden,
Enclosed by rose-red walls, great mulberry
    trees
Drowsed in the sun; and, cradled on their
    leaves,
The silk-worm spun its exquisite cocoons.

She watched them, and a sudden shining
    thought
Robed in a rainbow, like a statelier queen
Moved through her mind.
She dreamed of it all night,
And, in the morning, called three tongueless
    slaves
And told them to set up a secret loom
Within the palace. But to make quite sure

THE TORCH-BEARERS

The secret would be kept, their headless
  trunks
Were thrown at night into the Yellow River
Beyond those rose-red walls, in old Pekin.

Then, with her singing daughters, she went
  out
Into her garden, at the break of day,
To pluck the mulberries. In their hands they
  bore
Three gilded baskets, covered with green
  leaves
And, under those green leaves, if you had
  looked,
You would have seen three freshly severed
  heads.

They buried them in the garden, at the roots
Of those great brooding trees; and then they
  plucked
The mulberries, lifting hands like lotus-
  flowers
To the dark clusters under the broad leaves;

THE LAST VOYAGE

*And that is why their finger-tips, which
    glowed
Like delicate opal shells were stained so red.*

*But when they came into the house again,
Their baskets were still covered with green
    leaves,
And, under those broad leaves, if you had
    looked,
You would have seen, not mulberries, but
    cocoons.*

*Four thousand years ago, in old Pekin,
The queen and her two daughters wove and
    spun
Secretly, and embroidered their strange
    dreams
Through which there always ran one crimson
    thread
Twisting and trickling through the golds and
    blues
On those first silken miracles of Cathay.*

And they still kept the secret, while the world

Wondered whence those fantastic glories came
To smoulder on their walls.

                              And then they died.

The centuries passed, the mulberry trees lived
        on,
And still that secret passed from queen to
        queen
Like a celestial jewel closely locked
And guarded, in the treasury of a king.

And then, one summer night, a Princess woke
And heard the jargoning of great nightin-
        gales,
And opened her bright window to the stars,
Two thousand years ago, in old Pekin.

She heard the leaves breathe and the foun-
        tains flow,
Murmuring the same strange music as to-day.
And she was beautiful as an almond spray
In the first month of Spring.

THE LAST VOYAGE

                    Under her walls
A shadow stirred. She saw her lover stand
With face uplifted, through the dim blue
    gloom,
In old Pekin, two thousand years ago.

She let her silken ladder lightly down,
And fled with him into the boundless dusk
Of Asia, like a little fluttering moth
Out of a lighted window, into the night.

But, in her silken turban she had hidden
A cluster of mulberry leaves and silk-worm's
    eggs,
Because, she thought, when I am far away
In India, I will make a loom and weave
My happier memories into happier dawns
And turn my dreams to sunsets, as of old,
Two thousand years ago,
In old Pekin.

"And so the secret, as my father said,"
It was the lad's voice, not the murmuring
    bees,

In the dark lavender—"so the secret spread
Through the great world. . . . There is a
    curious song
I heard him sing it once as a nursery rhyme.
He often will hum it aloud, as we walk thro'
    the fields.

                 It tells of the magic
Wrapt up in the smallest of things."

                 "Eh! Eh! What a child!
Come, sing me that song," said the Mayor.

Then the boy, as his grey-green eyes, from
    easel to sitter,
Lifted and dropt, and his deft hand added a
    wrinkle,
And puffed those pouches under the Mayor's
    round eyes,
Chanted in undertone, almost as one in a
    dream,
Aloof and afar, these rhymes, through which
    I could hear
The lapse of the leaves, in the garden of old
    Pekin,

And the whisper of lovers through all the
    blind ages of death,
In a world beyond time, at one with the
    rhythmical whole.

Was it only the rush of the waves outside, and
    the pulse
Of the turbines, down in the dark, that shook
    the frame
Of the world? With what rhythmical pur-
    pose?

                At one with the pulse
Of the human heart, and the rhythm of tides
    and stars,
All speaking through each, in the light-foot
    lilt of a song,
Each speaking through all, and all wedded in
    music for me!

  A princess reigned in China
    Two thousand years ago. . . .
  And in her secret garden
    Great mulberries used to grow,

THE TORCH-BEARERS

With crooked boughs, and spreading
    leaves
    And deep dark roots below.

And out of those great dusky hearts
    In the heart of old Cathay,
She drew the sunset and the dawn . . .
    And smiled and stole away.
Two thousand years ago, it was,
    And it seems like yesterday.

Far off, on the deck of a ship, like a voice in
    a dream,
You think they will save her?
            Far off, in the thick of the storm,
Then, suddenly, close at hand, through the
    thunder of waves,
Like a voice in a dream replying,—Who are
    They?

X

Alone in his own cabin,
But never less lonely than when quite alone,
The poet invoked that other magic now,
Magic that, through a woven order of words,
A crafty arrangement of articulate sounds,
Could wake new values and suffuse his line
With a celestial wonder, till it shone
Like something captured from the eternal
    world,
Discovered, not composed; revealed, not
    made;
Rhythmical as the cosmos, with the pulse
Of natural law; yet, by that service, free;
A flawless and inevitable form,
A wingèd phrase of the perfect symphony
Dictated by the heart-beats of that love
Which moves the sun and stars. . . .
                    The sea went by
Thundering. He did not hear it. . . .
And now he turned the pages of his book

And tried to choose a cluster of lighter songs
For his first reading in that distant land. . . .
And, as he turned them over, he could see
Already, in thought, as through a magic
 window,
The thronged and radiant hall beside the lake
At Wellesley; or the doors of old Nassau,
With those bronze tigers, where the redcoats
 passed
Up the grey steps of memory, long ago.
He saw the tower that calls across the sea
To Magdalen; saw the crumbling stones they
 brought
From Oxford, stones incorporate now for ever
In the new walls that guard the eternal flame.
There was the true America that he loved
As Shelley loved it; there, and at old Yale,
Mother of men, to whom across the wave,
The denizens of the Mermaid Inn have flown
And found, once more, the Elizabethan fire;
There, and in those elm-shadowed whispering
 ways
At Cambridge, where John Harvard left the
 books

THE LAST VOYAGE

He brought from Cambridge, England, with
    the hope
That gleams, as freshly as the mayflower
    gleams,
Clear-cut in stone, above those gates of youth
In his own country, for all ages now:
When God had carried us safe to our New
    England;
When we had built our houses; made secure
The needs of life; established civil law;
And raised convenient places for God's wor-
    ship;
The next thing that we longed for was to
    advance
Knowledge, and hand it on from sire to son,
Dreading to leave our cause to the forgetful
When we shall lie in dust. . . .

                All these he saw,
And many another, thronged with the wel-
    coming light
Of friendship, far beyond the weltering flood;
And many a page of April song he turned,
But paused on one which seemed to whisper
    there

Of stranger powers than when he wrote it
     first;
Powers that with deeper magic, subtler spells,
Were moving round the ship, in air and sea,
And the deep ether, under the blind storm,
And his own voyaging soul; miraculous
     powers
That make and shape, sustain and guide the
     world.
He paused on this, and with a flickering
     smile,
Remembering how the careless lyric leapt
Once, from a boy's heart, like a blackbird's
     carol,
Out of a may-tree, murmured it anew.

Wizards

There's many a proud wizard in Araby and
     Egypt
  Can read the silver writing of the stars as
     they run;
And many a dark gypsy, with a pheasant in his
     knapsack,

Has gathered more by moonshine than
  wiser men have won;

But *I* know a Wizardry
  Can take a buried acorn
And whisper forests out of it, to tower against
  the sun.

There's many a magician in Bagdad and
  Benares
  Can read you—for a penny—what your fu-
  ture is to be;
And a flock of crazy prophets that by staring
  at a crystal
  Can fill it with more fancies than there's
  herring in the sea;

But *I* know a Wizardry
  Can break a freckled egg-shell
And shake a throstle out of it, in every haw-
  thorn-tree.

There's many a crafty alchemist in Mecca
  and Jerusalem;

And Michael Scott and Merlin were
    reckoned very wise;

But *I* know a Wizardry
    Can take a wisp of sun-fire
And round it to a planet, and roll it through
    the skies,
    With cities, and sea-ports, and little shining
    windows,
And hedgerows and gardens, and loving
    human eyes. . . .

Those verses would not serve his purpose now.
He had been asked for something they could
    read
At the ship's concert, in a night or two
If all went well. . . .
                The wireless news was full
Of armaments, and peace; of speeches flashed
From Washington and London; how to end
This armoured drag on 'progress.'
                        Long ago
He had written something—he remembered
    it—

That might seem fitting now. Was it too light,
Too hopeful for this war-stunned world of
    ours?
He paced the sheltered and deserted deck,
Alone. The verses echoed through his mind,
Recalling that old house above the sea,
The Golden Farm, hushed among tall blue
    pines,
Where first he wrote them down, in happier
    days.
Enriched with all those deeper undertones
Which none but he could hear, their silence
    flowed
Like an old memory of a boyish faith,
And a true purpose, ardent in him then
(When few would hear what all were preach-
    ing now,
Above the graves of twenty million dead!)
Thank God, he had written it long before,
    and joined
The voices that had failed. . . .
Salt, with that mockery, even as it smiled,
The very lightness of the music flowed
In its own harmony with this darkened hour;

And somewhere, deep in his unconscious
    mind,
Something was calling, calling through it
    all,—
Was it from France? What distant thunder
    broke?
Was it in Seventy? Yesterday? To-mor-
    row . . . ?
The verses flowed as lightly as the breath
Of the cool sea-wind playing round his brow;
And what both said was true, not to be
    mouthed
On any stage; but true as Nature here.
Although, outside, in darkness and in storm,
The Atlantic powers moved to their own
    strange dooms,
He walked the sail-screened deck, and that
    light breath
Of their vast tumult played its part as well
As the spray plays it, when the surge goes by.

   .   .   .   .

In the lost woods of Virginia, I found, at
    break of day,
An old colonial tavern, by a grass-grown way,

[104]

With white porch-pillars where the wild wis-
    teria grew,
Rosy with the dawn-flush, and misty with the
    dew

Now I'd been rambling in the woods to find
    the heart of things;
For all my mind was broken with the wicked
    ways of kings;
When a low wind shifted all that deep dim
    bloom,
And showed the golden name above the old
    Apollo Room

I had found the Raleigh Tavern, and the
    ghostly door was wide,
And I saw two shadows talking by the dark
    fire-side,
One was in a laced coat, and one in buff and
    blue,
And both of them were dead men, with faces
    that I knew.

[105]

Yes; there was Patrick Henry, in an oak arm-
chair,
With his long church-warden, and his fiery
mop of hair;
And he looked up, grimly: "Mr. Jefferson,"
he said,
"If Peace has come on earth at last, the Devil
must be dead.

"I'm Scots and Welsh; but if *he's* dead, and
left no heads to break,
I'm thinking that auld Nick will have a royal
Irish Wake;
For the Irish will be feelin' like the lad from
Venus-land,
With the olive-buds all sproutin' on the black-
thorn in his hand.

"There's just one hope! If half the world
agrees that war shall cease,
You'll have to call the Irish up to keep the
rest at peace
But England?"—"Ah," says Jefferson, "we'll
not say 'nay,'

THE LAST VOYAGE

If a Saxon chief, named Washington, should
    lead us on the way.

"When with Adams, Lee, and Stockton, that
    were England's blood and bone,
We stood for her own freedom, in the face of
    court and throne;
When we wrenched it from the Hessian; when
    we sealed our living creed
As the last red scripture, on the scroll of
    Runnymede;

There was many a golden Irish lad that fol-
    lowed our Saint George
With his tattered starving armies thro' the
    snows of Valley Forge. . . ."
"There's an auld cracked Bell," says Patrick,
    "and it talks in Shakespeare's tongue;
But the bones of the dead men remember and
    grow young.

As I saw him, in the darkness, looming up
    against the skies,

A great ghost, riding, with the battle in his
    eyes,
I have seen the New World rising, with the
    splendour of her stars,
And a Captain rides before her, that shall
    make an end of wars.

From his tomb by the Potōmac, on his proud
    white steed,
Well I know who comes to lead us, as of auld
    he used to lead,
And the drums of the morning up the Rappa-
    hannock roll,
'It's the Father of his country, and it's Eng-
    land's living soul.' "

*Then softly—very softly—while the shadows
    died away,
In the ancient Raleigh Tavern, at the dawn-
    ing of the day,
"By God's good grace," quoth Jefferson, "if
    both our hearts be true,
We, who split the world asunder, may unite
    the world anew."*

.   .   .   .

THE LAST VOYAGE

Far off, in France,
Through rolling mists, the desolate villages.
And lightning-blasted trees—and the long
*   road*
Where old Pasteur, all science left behind,
Went driving, driving, driving to the North,
Halting at wayside hospitals, hurrying on,
Seeking and searching like a questing hound,
With eyes of all too human agony, on,
On to the thunder of guns, his grey hair
*   flying,*
Like a new Lear, the terrible outcast King
Of human knowledge; but, in his bursting
*   heart,*
Only one cry, "My son! My son! My son!"

XI

The throb of the engine died. The rushing
    thunder
Of foam around the bows dissolved away.
The great ship drifted through a strange new
    hush.
Only the wash now of the slow deep seas
Against her towering flanks arose and fell
With that primæval sound the sea-gull heard
On lonely coasts,
Before the birth of man.

All that old mystery, with its rhythmic speech
Encompassed us again, while—for one child,
Out of the wide world's multitudes, one child
The lonely, vivid, quivering centre now
Of that vast round of empty sea and sky,
The concentrated powers of man held back
The Juggernaut wheels of death.

THE LAST VOYAGE

What voice was that?
Quivering with elfin ecstasy, far away,—
What child's tale, what deep legend of old
days,
What wounded nightingale lost in the dark
woods
Of Time, breathed its blind passion through
the storm:

"Where?" said the King,
"Oh, where? I have not found it."
"Here," said the dwarf,
And music echoed "here."
"This infinite circle hath no line to bound it,
Therefore its deep strange centre is every-
where.
Let the earth soar through heaven, that centre
abideth;
Or plunge to the pit, His covenant still
holds true.
In the heart of a dying bird, the Master
hideth;
In the soul of a King," said the dwarf, "and
in my soul, too."

[111]

Stillness—the dreadful waiting—and our ship,
With that one child, the centre of all things
    now. . . .

    .   .   .   .

In a hushed corner of the sail-screened deck
The astronomer and the old Franciscan padre
Talked in low voices of that same strange
    theme,—
Time, Space, and their infinitudes which
    make
Each point the centre of all. This flying mo-
    ment
Infinitudes being equal, stands midway
Between the past and future; and this child
Infinitudes being equal, lies midway
Between the abyss of stars, and those dark
    gulfs
Wherein the electrons wheel. So Space and
    Time,
As Plato, Hegel, Einstein, groped to see,
Dissolve into a shadow of man's mind;
And the one God is ever Here and Now,
God in the heights, and on ten thousand altars,

THE LAST VOYAGE

Revealed to man, when the blind doors are
 opened,
And the Bread broken, and the incarnate
 Word
Breathes thro' the worlds which veil Him
 from our sight,
Est enim Corpus Meum.

XII

The ship rocked idly.

    The surgeon, like a shadow,
With grey set face, came out through a
 shadowy door,
Quickly, on to the deck. He did not see us.
 He drew
A deep breath of the cold night air.

      The padre
Approached him.

    "Is all well?"

     He shook his head.
"Not——"

   "Worse than any one thought. It
 was too late.
The child is dead."

    There was a stifled cry below,
Faint, far, as the cry of a sea-mew, blindly
 astray
In the black night. . . .

Then, muffling it, the indifferent engines
    throbbed
And the great ship moved on its way again,
Steered by its earth-bound compass.
                   "Poor, poor mother,"
The padre whispered.
                   And the foam swept by.

"Padre, I have no faith in any creed.
For me,—at death—the human life goes out
Like a snuffed candle. But, if there's any
    word
Of comfort you can give to that poor woman,
For God's sake go and speak to her."
                   "Not yet,"
The padre murmured. "No, not yet, my
    friend."
And, though he said no more, his inmost
    thoughts
Breathed through me, like a voice.
                 "The ship moves on,
To its own goal. It takes us all one way,
Living and dead; and the foam speaks of
    speed.

And the dark planet spins on its own course
Bearing us back. Look up. The stars are
    still,
Fixed, fixed and still; yet they, too, speak of
    speed.

And neither ship nor stars can move one inch
The nearer to the final end of man,
Ours is a deeper goal, beyond this dream
Of Time and Space! . . .
                    Neither the speeding ship
Nor all the rushing seas can move my mind
From its fixed centre. That great arch of sky
Still keeps us in the centre of its round
Wherever we move; nor can we ever escape
From that dread point, wherein each blade of
    grass,
Each leaf, each flower, each separate strug-
    gling life,
As though beneath the intense blue lens of
    heaven
It lay alone, concentrates on itself
The gaze of That which only and ever exists
In its own right, beyond. . . ."

THE LAST VOYAGE

          "What lies beyond?
Science has struck a death-blow at the heart
Of all that you believe."
                      "I answer that
Out of the mouth of Science." . . .

   .   .   .   .

                    There, at once
The scene dissolved. The veils of Time and
    Space
Like a blind mist rolled back.
I saw the lights of Paris. I heard the roar
Of trafficking streets. The Mazarin palace
    flung
Its doors wide open, and my ghost passed
    through.

There, in that glittering hall, I saw and heard
The Academy of France with all its guests
Assembled to instal their new immortal,
Louis Pasteur, in a death-vacated chair.

It was no dream. The green embroidered
    coats

Of those who were to live for ever gleamed
Before me; and, among them, in a haze
Of starry decorations, their proud guests,
Plump statesmen, rosy senators, bowed and
    shrugged,
Replete with self-importance. At their sides
Bejewelled wives and white-armed daughters
    raised
Their rounded mouths like desperate chor-
    isters
Trying in vain to pierce the chattering din
And reach a neighbour's ear; for that bright
    Babel
Sounded as though the reservoirs of speech
In great Gargantua's Dictionary had burst,
And all the words in the world were pouring
    out
In cataracts, over the drowning eyes of
    thought.
And yet, it was truth itself they had come to
    crown
In one whom France had bound to the lonely
    peak

THE LAST VOYAGE

Where once Prometheus hung, and the eagle
    of hate
Savaged his heart; till a world elsewhere had
    caught
The torch that he flung thro' darkness, and
    forced his land
To acknowledge his truth at last.
                    And so they acclaimed
An immortal, Louis Pasteur.

A strange, dramatic scene, the antiphonal hour
To an hour when Huxley, at Oxford, struck
    his blow
For Science, at smooth-tongued Wilberforce.
              Here, in France,
The parts were subtly reversed.
                 In the chief place,
Renan sat smiling, ironically secure
As President of the Academy of France;
Renan, still hearing those deep sunken bells
Of the celestial City, faint and far,
Like the deep chimes of that drowned City
    of Is

THE TORCH-BEARERS

The Breton sailors hear; Renan, so sure
That Science had dissolved his ancient faith
Into a rose-pink myth, would now receive
This uncrowned King of Science, and crown
     him there
Pasteur, the new immortal. . . .

Renan, superior to all folk-lore now;
The first of pseudo-moderns, sure, so sure,
That Science was his ally through all change,
Had come to hear this master of clear-cut fact
Confirm his musical dilettante prose,
And prove once more that Reason leads the
     mind
Into a creedless twilight, touching all
That most concerns man, his purpose here,
The meaning of the world, and his last end.

Slight analyst of Christ; fond amateur
Of Reason, he sat there, in state, and smiled,
Hatching a witty phrase for his own speech
Which should lead subtly on to a minor chord
Of vague emotion, and die on the hushed air
Like wordless music.

THE LAST VOYAGE

> On his right, Pasteur,
The master of all those hard and clear-cut
    facts,
The pioneer, a poor old, time-worn man,
Bent his grey head, and clutched his manu-
    script,
With trembling hands, as one who felt half-
    dazed
At thus emerging from the lonely night
Of his long fight for truth, into this blaze
Of glory. A labouring miner who has cut
Through the sheer rock in darkness, and
    emerged
On bright Olympus to the applause of gods
Were not bewildered more. . . .
What should he say? How thank them for
    their aid,
Now all was over and his brows were crowned
With light and victory? Victory? Not till
    death!
Crowned? Not by these, but by the stubborn
    hands
Of his own proven facts, in the lying face

Of those that would have stoned him, stoned
    to kill.

How should he tell them when he rose to
    speak

The things that he had learned in that long
    night,

The facts, the cold realities he had proved,

Cold as cold iron through the hands and
    feet. . . .

Renan sat smiling there.

First, as of use and wont, Pasteur must speak

In eulogy of the dead, must pay his debt

To Littré, his forerunner, who had been

The chief disciple of Comte, but lost, at last,

Even that earth-bound faith his master held

In Man, whose godhead dies with his own sun,

And perishes with his planet. . . .

Littré, for whom the visible, tangible world

Was all; but whose departure from it now

Into a world invisible, left one chair

Among the immortals (O, ironic Death!)

Thus vacant for the bent and grey Pasteur.

THE LAST VOYAGE

How could he tell them of the thing he saw
Three days ago, upon the dead man's
    wall. . . .

How could he tell a cynical throng like this
Of what he saw when, anxious for the truth,
In its minutest detail, ere he spoke
His mind on Littré, he had visited
The dead man's house, a labourer's cottage
    rather,
And seen the lowly garden of his delight,
The lilac-tree beneath whose boughs he read
La Fontaine, Horace, Vergil; and that room
Whence, labouring, with the midnight lamp
    unquenched,
He heard the nightingale and skylark blend
Their notes in one strange carol of night and
    day.
There, on the bare cold wall of that small
    room,
Where Littré worked . . . that crucifix.
                        Not his own. . . .
His wife's, and yet, O doubly then his
    own. . . .

Far off, through Time and Space, what music
    breathed,

Quench not in any shrine
The smouldering storax. In no human
    heart
Quench what love kindled. Faintly though
    it shine,
Not till it wholly dies the gods depart.

Courage, O conquering soul.
For all the boundless night that whelms thee
    now
Though suns and stars into oblivion roll,
The gods abide, and of their race art thou.

The moment had arrived, and he must speak.
A brief and quiet throbbing of acclaim
Broke the deep hush. Pasteur was on his feet,
Nervous and awkward, paler than his wont.
The Academician's green embroidered coat
Felt new and strange. Across his breast he
    wore
The cordon of the Legion. . . .

THE LAST VOYAGE

Far, how far,
Beyond those walls, a child was walking now
Clasping his father's hand. The straight old
*   man,*
One of Napoleon's veterans . . . murmuring
*   streams. . . .*
Blue hills, how far. . . .

All this was in his voice,
Welled up in him from deep unconscious
    springs,
As he began to speak . . . of Littré first,
And his achievements in the positive realm
Of Science. To all these he paid his debt
From a full mind. Then, suddenly, he
    paused,
And the old grey man that had so long ex-
    plored
Those infinitesimal worlds beneath the lens
Of Science, raised his head.

He did not see
The throng who had come to hear the world
    explained
In terms of dust, the greater by the less,
Revoking the first law of their own thought

In intellectual arrogance. His voice
Rang clearly out. *"At the chief point of all
This positivism fails."*

                    The hush grew tense.
Renan sat smiling there.

                       *"Because it fails
To take into account another fact,
The most important, positive fact of all,
The Infinite. . .*

*I can give no formula
For its expression here."*

                    Far off, in time
A murmur from Stagira, gathering strength,
And depth from Aquin, breathed, *The order
    of Nature
Is not the order of Thought; for we explain
The first things by the last. The maximum
    genus
Which is both first and last, explains what man
Finds least and lowest.* It struck—to the very
    heart
Of Darwin's failure. They would not under-
    stand,

Though he spoke volumes. He must choose
    his terms.
Renan sat smiling there. It was the Age
Of Doubt. True thought was dead. They
    did not hear,
They could not read one thought except their
    own.
Pasteur would choose and use their own vague
    terms
And still refute that smile.
                      "What is beyond?"
His voice rang out, as from a bursting heart,
Deep, struggling to keep back those deepest
    things
That simple minds know best, because ex-
    tremes
In these things meet, as God in childhood
    dwells.
What is beyond? Trace man into the dust
Descend into those infinitesimal gulfs
Of microscopic life; or mount through Space
And see ten thousand universes move
In order round you; never shall you escape
From that one question every child can ask,

And answer, out of the Light that dwells
    within.
*"'What is beyond?' The mind of man, urged
    on
By an invincible passion, never will cease
To ask, What is beyond?*

                    Vain to reply
*'Unbounded Time and Space, unbounded
    grandeur,'*
Vague phrases, for the one most absolute Fact.
He who discerns the Infinite in his heart
Transcends all human science, and affirms
More of the supernatural than is found
In all the miracles.

                 It is forced upon us.
None can avoid it. Everywhere in the world
Behind all facts, this ultimate mystery,
Remains, incomprehensible.

                 When this vision
*Dawns on our human minds, we can but
    kneel."*

Renan still smiled that suave complacent smile
Of *a priori* doubt and self-conceit,

THE LAST VOYAGE

So sure that, intellectually, he held
A more Olympian height, wherefrom to lisp
"Come unto me, all ye that are most witty
Refresh my soul with epigrams."

                                        Pasteur

Lowered his voice a little, and spoke on.

"The idea of God—what is it but the sense
Of this dark mystery of the Infinite One;
Whereby, deep down in every human heart,
The supernatural dwells.
As long as this eternal mystery weighs
On human thought, so long mankind will
    build
Temples to heaven, whether their God be
    known
As Brahma, Allah, Jahveh, or as Christ.
And, on the pavement of those temples, men
Will be found kneeling, prostrate, all their
    world
Annihilated, and in dust around them,
Before this thought, the Infinite."

                              For a moment,

The rows of listening faces faded out:

And he, Pasteur, who had come to speak in
    praise
Of positive science, and himself was crowned
For his discoveries in the dwindling gulf
Of infinitesimal things, no longer knew
If Renan smiled or not. He cared no more.
The voice with which he spoke was not his
    own.
And, in the expectant silence, there were those
Who heard the thought he did not choose to
    speak:

"This Infinite is not the mere unbounded,
Dying away through its unclosed horizons
Into an endless void. The highest name,
And so the truest, given to it on earth,
Is that of the Perfect. This, indeed, is bound
By its own character; and discerned, though
    dimly,
And only in fragments, through the beauty of
    Art;
But, sometimes, more completely, in those
    hours
When, for a vision of right, the spirit of man

[130]

THE LAST VOYAGE

Stands up alone against a mocking world
And drinks defeat like victory.

                              Once, at least,
Well nigh two thousand years ago, out-
    stretched
On the one frame that, pointing opposite ways,
Can image still that ultimate paradox
Where at the centre of the whole creation
The one impossible Fact sustains the whole,
And, through the universe, on His cross of
    law,
The Maker still redeems what He has made,
The Infinite spoke to man."

                              Then, in a voice
Filled with all this, as at the appointed note
A blind musician is caught up and forced
By the invisible orchestra around him
To play his part, his words rang out again,—

"Blessed is he who bears within his breast
A God, a true ideal, and obeys it,
Whether through Art, or Science, or a life
Of simple goodness. There is the deep source

THE TORCH-BEARERS

*Of all good thoughts and actions. It reflects
Light from the Infinite."*

He ceased, and took his place. The crowd
    was hushed.
Renan, still smiling, turned his papers over,
And then, still seated, in his loftier chair,
As President, cooed his airy answer out,
An answer couched in terms with but one aim,
To ensure that all his light ironic praise
Should fall, as from an intellectual height,
On this up-struggling genius.
                        "Sir, we know
That we are hardly competent to judge
The glory of your work," he cooed and
    purred.
"But there's a greatness, quite apart from
    this—
Which our experience of the human mind
Must recognise at once." The smile con-
    veyed,
The very tone and gesture seemed to assume,
That this most special greatness was his own,
And gave him power to judge its lesser forms.

[132]

THE LAST VOYAGE

"We recognise this greatness in the work
Of widely various minds. In Galileo,
Molière, Pascal, Michael Angelo,
We see it shining,—something that can give
To poets, the sublime; to orators
Enchantment; to philosophers the depths
Of reason; and to scientists the power
Of—divination.

            Sir, that common fount
Of true and beautiful work; that sacred fire;
That indefinable truth which kindles Art,
Literature, Science, we have found in *you*.
Sir, it is genius. No one ever walked
So surely through the elemental maze
Of Nature. Sir, your scientific life
Is like" (he smiled) "a little luminous tract
In the great night of the Infinitesimal,
The last abyss, where life itself is born.
But Truth, sir, Truth, sir, is a great coquette.
She shrinks from too much passion, and will
    prove
More yielding, sometimes, to indifference."
(The very cadence murmured 'even as
    mine.')

"She escapes when she seems caught, but gives
    herself
To those who wait; reveals her loveliness
When our farewells are said; but goes her way
Inexorably, when loved with too much
    fervour. . . ."

"Beautiful, beautiful," breathed the senators'
    wives;
And all their daughters' eyes were on his face.

Then, by a swift suggestion, subtly masked
In compliment, he indirectly affirmed
His loftier sphere of abstract intellect.

"Nature, sir, is plebeian. She insists
On labour; calloused hands and care-worn
    brows.
You are happy in your certainties. For me
There is a charm in doubt. We shall not find
The secret of that exquisite enigma

[134]

Which so torments and charms us. Need we
    care,
When even the hem of the garment we have
    raised
Reveals such beauty. Allow me to recall
Your own discovery, sir, of right and left
Tartaric acids. Are there not some minds
That, like those acids, never can unite;
Minds, that, to use your own comparison, sir,
Are like the gloves required by opposite
    hands;
Minds that can meet, but never be inter-
    changed,
Though both are needed.

                   Sir, you look beyond,
And you discern a light in death itself.
Death, which to Littré, was a function
    only. . . ."

(O, words, words, words, how emptily they
    flowed
Through the deep aching mind of old
    Pasteur!)

[135]

"The last and quietest function of our flesh,
Death seems to me most odious and insane
When its cold touch is laid upon the heart
Of virtue and of genius. In great souls
There is a voice which cries unceasingly
'Goodness and Truth must ever be your goal.
Sacrifice all to these.' But, when we obey
That siren voice and reach the trysting-tree
Where the reward should wait us, there is
        nothing.
The vague Consoler fails us at the last.
Philosophy, which had promised us the key
To the dark riddle of death, averts her face,
Muttering a lame apology, like a man
Avoiding an old friend who asks for alms.
The bright ideal that had led us on
To the thin fringe of the last air we breathe
Dies like a marsh-light at the supreme hour
When we most need and look for it. Nature's
        end
Has been attained; a cold experiment made;
Then, with a harlot's gesture, the Enchantress
Leaves our senility to the hooting birds
Of darkness. I agree, sir, that we owe,

And ought to pay, our little debt of virtue
To the implacable Power that treats us thus;
But, while we pay it, sir, I also think
We have the right, upon our own account,
To add a little irony."

                    Assured
That he had proved his own pre-eminent wit,
Renan would say no more.

                    Pasteur's grey head
Was bowed. He did not smile. He thought
    it strange,
That men should use their irony on a theme
Which had so haunted many a master-mind
And filled with light so many a simple heart.

The applause grew faint and distant, like a
    dream.
He hardly knew what followed; for he heard
With his own innermost mind, another voice
That tingled through the gulfs of Space and
    Time
Like star-light, the far voice of one who
    walked

Through Konigsberg,—a small dry clock-
    work man,
Angular as his own cocked hat, and brown
As his own coffee, who, while his clock-work
    feet
Clicked through the market-place so punc-
    tually
That townsmen told the time by him, would
    range
In his own thought, through kingdoms beyond
    Time;
And, though the clouds of that high region
    swept
Around him often, through their rifts he
    caught
Gleams of eternal radiance. Though he
    failed
To build a mightier fane with his own hands,
Unconsciously, and even against his will,
He still confirmed the strength of that which
    stands
In saecula saeculorum, while he groped
Through Nature, and discovered in the laws
Of his dark mind, an end above her own;

And higher yet, an end where both accord,
And bear one witness to the Supreme Good;
One vast synthetic witness, from the law
That bowed his head beneath the wheeling
    stars,
And from the deeper law in man's own soul,
Whose strange, imperative whisper, far
    within,
Affirmed, 'Thou *must,* despite thine own de-
    sires,
Though all thy hopes be shattered by this
    choice,
Thou *must* uphold the right; and, in thy
    power
To hear this absolute whisper and defy
What seemed the wheel of Nature, thou hast
    proved
Thy freedom, in a loftier order now;
Proved to thine own true self the eternal
    strength
Of its true fortress, founded on a rock
In kingdoms of reality, beyond
This world of fleeting shadows. Thou hast
    proved

THE TORCH-BEARERS

Though blind men cannot see, or deaf men
    hear,
The three great affirmations which alone
Can save mankind from utter chaos now,
God, Freedom, Immortality.'

XIII

In a small cabin, lit by a single lamp,
The poet, rapt and tense, had dropt his pen.
Whose Mind dictated, or whose Will com-
    pelled
His half-unconscious music? Not his own.
He had written as one that listens and strains
    long
To hear a distant harmony. It was there:
One *motif* in the world-wide symphony;
A form of truth, eternal in the heavens,
Not to be made with hands, composed by
    minds,
But to be found, discovered, phrase by phrase,
In its abiding Beauty.
                        Could he grasp
The whole—record its half-remembered notes,
Each by a golden logic leading on
And up, to a new wonder; Music then
Had opened the last blinding doors of knowl-
    edge,

And shrivelled him in that last consummate
    splendour,
The Beatific Vision.

Death, that had hushed the ship for half an
    hour
As with a strange new presence, was to him
No stranger, but a comrade of his thought,
Touching him daily, whispering in his ear;
And all his pity for that stricken child
Only renewed a memory and a pang,
Only confirmed a sad foreknowledge now
That ached in him from boyhood.
                   He knew it then;
And, afterwards, he knew that not till Death
Struck and the mortal body of one he loved
Lay there before him in a strange content,
So still that, by a deeper contrast now,
With the imperceptible gathering of the dark,
And the unseen moving air, it seemed to
    breathe;
Never till one rapt form, in that strange bliss
Lay smiling, through the mists of his own
    grief,

THE LAST VOYAGE

At an invisible heaven, had he discerned
That what he loved was separable from earth.
There, though the mortal body had not yet
    lost
One shining atom in its frozen sleep,
And the still exquisite face looked up, un-
    changed,
From those untroubled waves of lustrous hair;
Something had vanished utterly from the
    world,
Whose lightest whisper, half an hour ago
Out-valued all earth's kingdoms. Stocks and
    stones
Endured. Could this, then, perish like a flash
Struck from a flint. The mortal shell re-
    mained.
The cold and stiffening fingers could be
    touched,
Claspt, kissed, and idly stained with human
    tears;
But, even in that last agony he knew
That he stretched out his blind imploring
    hands
To an immortal fugitive.

Then, oh then,
He clutched at hints and whispers from be-
yond,
Messages from the dead! He turned a page
And read, as he remembered his own grief,
Strange words that love had whispered to him
then:

Never again the heaven in those clear eyes,
  The dew, the glory, and the unfaltering
    love;
Never again those stars of Paradise
  Which watched my labouring darkness
    from above;
Never again, O never again, the look
  That like the sunlight blessed me unaware;
Innocence wiser far than any book,
  And silent faith out-soaring any prayer.

Never again the hand that moved in mine
  With that quick pulse when love could find
    no word,
Never again the white robe and the shrine

[144]

THE LAST VOYAGE

And those dear songs that none but I have
heard,
Laughed out at dawn, lost songs of childish
years,
Remembered now, in darkness, and blind
tears.

II

Every morning, a bird
    Alights on the topmost bough of the
        silver birch-tree
Between the house and the lake,
    And sits there alone for an hour
Looking in, looking in at my window.

It may be a blackbird or thrush,
    But the light at that hour is deceptive.
I only know it is different from all other
        birds.

It utters no cry, no song.
    I have never seen it alighting.

[145]

THE TORCH-BEARERS

And yet, when the sky is like apple-bloom
    over the lake,
  And my eyes have grown used to the light,
It is always there,
  At the very same time by the sun,
A little while after daybreak.
  It always chooses the same bare bough,
And it sits there alone, for an hour,
  Looking in, looking in at my window.

Is it so that our lost ones return
  With eager inquisitive love,
Using strange eyes for an hour,
  To glance through an open window
And discover how much we have changed?

It is daybreak now,
  And the bird is not here;
But strange and terrible thoughts bewilder
    one's mind
  Before it is half-awake,
And my heart sinks,
  With fear of some evil that may have be-
    fallen my bird.

[146]

THE LAST VOYAGE

Wings rustle.
 The topmost bough of the silver birch-
  tree
Suddenly dips and sways
 And all is well.
Dark on an apple-bloom sky
 A silent bird
Sits there alone, looking in,
 Looking in, looking in at my window.

III

Messages? Like the pagans of old time
 I grope for messages in the flight of birds;
A book that opens at your favourite rhyme;
 A page turned down; a passing stranger's
  words;
Till in this wide world's ordered mazes now
 No leaf can fall, no bird can come and go,
No ray of sunlight touch a child's fair brow,
 But with a secret meaning that I know.

I prayed that, if you could, you'd let me hear
 The name you gave me, and none other
  knew;

THE TORCH-BEARERS

And that same evening, standing by my chair,
A child, on tiptoe, whispered it for you;
A stranger's child, not knowing what she said
Whispered that happy name. I bowed my
head.

At times, it almost seemed as though a light
Could shine through rifts in the dissolving
veil
Of Nature, and strange meanings glimmered
through
That others could not see. Even now, he
heard
And saw, beyond all hearing and all sight,
Messages flung through darkness from afar,
Wild hieroglyphic hints, like those quick cries
Of prophecy, those crooked lightnings flashed
Through Pagan skies, before the Word took
flesh
And the Infinite God performed that only Act
Wherein He fully expressed infinitude
And rounded His own infinite universe
By being born of that which He had made.

THE LAST VOYAGE

                              In vain he strove
To seize and hold, through all the shows of
    Time,
The intolerable messenger of God,
Who, cloaked with sordid shreds of mortal
    clay,
Disguised in rags of this material world
Burns thro' the veil and smoulders thro' the
    cloud,
As beauty everywhere; yet at one touch
Shrivels the wrestling sinews of the mind.

  Messages,—from the dead?
  Thou has not heard them? No;
  Nor shalt thou ever hear
  What whisperings come and go.
  But, when thou hast bowed thy head
  In the quietude of despair
  When thou hast ceased to listen,
  A meaning shall draw near
  And startle thee like a light,
  From valleys of surprise
  Opening, out of sight
  Behind thee; for 'tis written

THE TORCH-BEARERS

They must not meet thine eyes.
Between the effect and cause
They dare not intervene.
From the unseen to the seen
Their roads are Nature's laws;
But, through them, they can breathe
What none could speak aloud;
And quietly inter-wreathe
Through sea-wave and white cloud
Strange gleams of loveliness
Whose deep unearthly drift
Thou couldst not even guess;
Light that no eyes can see;
Music no ear hath heard;
Till they strike home to thee
Through star and sunset rift
Or the cry of a wandering bird;
And where the rainbow shone
Across unshadowing skies,
Clear as through tear-lashed eyes
Thy love smiles, and is gone.

Rememberest thou that hour,
Under the naked boughs,

THE LAST VOYAGE

When, desolate and alone,
Returning to thy house,
Thou stoodst amazed to find
Dropt on the lintel-stone
Which thou hadst left so bare,
A radiant dew-drenched flower—
And thou couldst never know
Whose hand had dropt it there,
Fragrant and white as snow,
To save thy soul from hell?
Yet, in thy deepest mind,
Thou *didst* know, and know well.

Not thine to understand
How the two worlds accord,—
The will of Love, our Lord,
With this dark wheel of Time.
Yet thou didst hear them chime
Like one deep Sanctus bell
For the pure Host revealed
In the exquisite miracle
Of that white chance-dropt flower;
A flower from a known field,
And dropt by a mortal hand;

But, breathing its wild dew,
O, simply as tears flow,
Thou didst most surely know
The hand from which it fell
Was thy lost angel's, too.

The implacable law was there; and yet he
    knew
That, though the world, like music, moved in
    law
Its notes are not mechanical, but express
The Spirit of its Creator, who unfolds
His infinite purpose and compassionate will
With every touch, finding in law itself
His perfect freedom to extemporise
Fugues that redeem the chords that went
    astray,
Tones that transfigure like the touch of Christ,
And providential harmonies that receive
The breaking wave of melody into a tide
Of deeper power and purpose, where it wakes
Into new life.
           There's not a wisp of cloud
Or flickering shadow of a summer leaf

But lends its delicate note to the infinite range
Of possible modulations, the reserves
From which, at need, the Master-Player
draws
His natural-supernatural power to glide,
In absolute freedom, through the laws He
made;
To keep them, yet transcend them; and so
work
His living Personal Will.
                                An earth-bound age,
This age of the machine, may see in law
That mechano-morphic image of itself,
A blind monistic web, wherein mankind
Is jerked by strings like crudest jack-a-clocks.
As though the death-watch, ticking in the
wood
Under the keys of the organ, should declare
That Bach's great choral Passion meant no
more
Than clicking wooden keys, and that an eye
Which sees their patterned movements from
below
Sees the bleak naked truth, and can despise

The vague hypothesis of a Mind beyond
The wooden frame-work. But in that deep
    realm
Infinite, inexhaustible, though law
Still runs through all, the Music-maker still
Works through the law His own deep
    miracles;
For, as the will of man can lift the hand
Against the pull of the planet, higher laws
Can sway each lesser system to new ends.
Height over height of law, through all the
    grades
Of hierarchic heaven, the law still runs;
Though every height, in its new splendour
    seems
An utter miracle to the grade below;
The flower a miracle to the lifeless earth;
The moth a miracle to the wingless flower;
Man, on his knees, in dark cathedral aisles,
A miracle to the burning jungle-beast;
And the unconditioned Power that made them
    all
A miracle to His universe. Thus the law
Climbs to His freedom, and sets the spirit free

[154]

THE LAST VOYAGE

Which by earth's dull mechanic law seemed
    bound;
For law itself, through its own changelessness,
Being steadfast as the memory of God,
Is Freedom's only surety, and the road
Whereon alone the spirit of man has power
To choose that goal and walk with surety to it,
Beyond the flaming ramparts of this world.
So let the new monistic moderns take
Music for clue and golden analogue,
Not that blind web of wooden puppetry
Pulled by material strings;
But Music, with its infinite subtlety,
Moving the soul, as when love speaks to love
In silence.
        This deep constancy of law
What is it but the covenant of our God
That His eternal Memory will retain
All that has ever been, or yet shall be;
The unchangeable scroll of judgment that has
    lost
No vanished sun, no atom, in the mists
Of all the endless ages.
             (Far away

THE TORCH-BEARERS

A voice breathed, 'not one bird or leaf can fall
Beyond your Father's care.')
                              The implacable law
Is God's own seal on all that we hold dear;
For Resurrection, in the eternal Mind,
Is but Remembrance.   Into the world-wide
    light
Of Memory there, His Memory, not our own,
Our dead shall rise, out of the gulfing grave
Of Time, out of that blind forgetful deep,
With all their own lost memories in their eyes,
In an eternal region.
                        Then shall law,
(Law that has never broken one frail link
In its long chain; the seeming callous law
Whose cruelty closed the melody of each life,
And gave it form by closing it) appear
As Love at last, whereby the melody lives
In its own form for ever. . . .
                        With trembling hands
He turned the pages of that worn old script
He wrote so long ago, unconscious then
Of all the meaning that those words might
    hold.

THE LAST VOYAGE

Messages from the dead! He read, through
    tears,—
And there was one that moved like light in
    light
Before me there,—Love, human and divine,
That can exalt all weakness into power,—
Whispering, 'Take this deathless torch of
    song,'
Whispering, but with such faith that even I
Might call on Love to guide me, while I sang
Of those who caught the pure Promethean fire
One from another, each crying as he went
    down
To one that waited, crowned with youth and
    joy,
'Take thou the splendour. Carry it out of
    sight,
Into the great new age I must not know,
Into the great new realm I must not tread.'

XIV

In her dark cabin, the stricken mother knelt
By her dead child. Only ten yards away
In a dark cabin, a happier mother lulled
Her wakeful child to sleep; a rose-lipped
    child
Hugging a Teddy Bear, and strangely alive
To the unwonted silence of the ship.
Tell me another rhyme, then, and I'll try.
Please, mummy, the one about buckets and
    ships at sea.
The childish treble piped; and, answering it,
The mother's low soprano quietly crooned:

    Buckets and spades and a ship at sea
    Are very fine things in their way, maybe;
    And the woods look gay when the boughs
        are green,
    But the very best things have never been
        seen.

THE LAST VOYAGE

Nobody ever has weighed or caught
One glimpse, with his eyes, of your happiest
thought;
Or walked in white where your prayers
have been,
*For the very best things have never been
seen.*

There is much to be said for an ark, one
feels;
And almost as much for a horse on wheels;
And the king has a crown (and so has the
queen)
*But the very best things have never been
seen.*

When the great winds blow and the sere
leaves fall,
Hide close, little elf, we can laugh at them
all!
If I whisper one word you will know what
I mean;
*For the very best things have never been
seen.*

THE TORCH-BEARERS

One word whispered—strange, across the
  night
Deeper than any wireless message thrilled
The soundless voice of Aquin, one deep chord
Sustaining that light song with undertones
Profound as death, in the innermost heart of
  the world:

> *Visus, tactus, gustus,*
>   *In te fallitur.*
> *Sed auditu solo*
>   *Tuto creditur.*

And then the voice of the child again, "One
  more,
Please—please—one more—and then I'll go
  to sleep.
The one about the grey wall in the garden
The wall that had a picture on it, mummy,
A picture that had turned into a window,
And showed a lovely face."

       "Ah, yes, I know,
The Invisible Garden. Cuddle your head
  down

THE LAST VOYAGE

Here, on the pillow, then; and I will say it;
Now, close your eyes." And softly as the
    sound
Of fir-trees, when a breath at evening moves
Their nodding plumes in a little sheltered glen
Among the lonely hills, the mother crooned:

You have never seen my garden,—
    There are strange roses here,—
Five beds of sunset roses,
    Afloat on the soft air.

Once in this happy garden,
    A dial marked the hours.
But there is no more sorrow
    Among my thoughtful flowers.

And, at the end of the garden,
    Clasped on the rose-grey wall,
I see, above the roses,
    The loveliest flower of all,—

A plaque enwreathed with sunset,
    White on a ground of blue,

THE TORCH-BEARERS

No della Robbia dreamed it;
   For here all dreams come true;

No plaque, but a bright window,
   In a wall of the unseen,
And one that sits within it,
   A maiden and a queen.

Pure white on blue, Our Lady,
   The Child upon her knee,
Stretching his little arms out,
   To pluck more flowers for me;

Stretching his arms out gently,
   To tall celestial flowers. . . .

The dial marks no longer the shadow of
       passing hours. . . .

The sunset quietly deepens,
   The night will soon be here.
The stars will see my roses
   Afloat on the soft air.

THE LAST VOYAGE

I am not afraid of darkness
   All mercy and all grace
Are shining through that window.
   And I shall see her face.

   You have never seen my garden. . . .

Hush! Fast asleep! 'Good night, dear chick,
   good night!'
And, in that other room—*Asleep! Asleep!*
(*Through streaming tears*) *'Good night, dear*
   heart, good night!'

XV

The turbines throbbed. The huge Atlantic
    surge
Went seething past the port-holes. All was
    dark.
I heard the ship's bell ringing in the night,
The cry of the watch, "All's well." But all
    night long
I faced that mystery of a vaster deep
Whereon no mortal mind can ever sail
To any haven, till it dares embark
On yet another Ship, and be enclosed,
Cabined, confined, by bulwarks that shut out
The vastness that would drown it.

                      As a man
Must shape a cup to drink from, so the mind
Must use its finite symbols to enclose
The eternal vintage of the infinite truth;
Whereof one little draught enlightens more
Than all that human arrogance must lose
If with its naked hands it madly attempt

THE LAST VOYAGE

To grasp the rushing flood. It was for this
God made His finite creatures, and enclosed
Our human love in forms of roseate flesh,
That we might slowly learn, with human eyes,
To spell His infinite meanings; till, at last,
As when a child has learned to walk, it needs
No fettering aid; or when the Temple is built
And the strong pillars between the cherubim
Support the cedar roofs, o'erlaid with gold,
The mortal scaffoldings where the masons
    worked
Are stripped away, and man's immortal soul,
Its wings full-grown, its elementary laws
All mastered, stands up radiant in the light
Of heaven, to share the Godhead of His love,
And serve with Him, in power.
                There, only there
In that deep inner kingdom which the fool
Accounts a world of dreams, abides the truth.
Yet man still seeks it on the dwindling road
Where Science traces great things back to less
Till all runs out in nothing, which the fool
Accounts the sole reality,—as of old.
Reality and Reality,—how we grope

[165]

And clutch at shadows in the shadowy flux
Of the unsubstantial universe, O God,
There was a time when Science walked on
    earth
And found it "solid"; looked on the blind bulk
Of matter, as the one sure final stuff
Which, through all change, endured, im-
    perishable;
While that invisible thought which fills no
    space,
And is not weighed or measured, and that
    strange Ego
Which, while it lives, through every bodily
    change,
Remembers and controls, and half-creates
The little sensuous scheme of colour and
    sound
We call our world, that central, personal *I,*
Can vanish utterly. . . .
O, for a true Copernicus of the mind
Who shall reverse this mockery. As of old,
Men thought their planet was the central stage
Of the universal drama, fixed and flat,
And found it whirling, like a pellet of dust

[166]

THE LAST VOYAGE

Through boundless night, so now—this earth,
    this flesh,
This matter again dissolves, dissolves, dis-
    solves,
Melts at a more than mortal Hamlet's cry,
Into electric systems, whirling coils
Of protons and electrons; which, at last
Under the scrutiny of the invisible mind
Are merged into the invisible world again
And rest with all their bodiless movements
    there
On That which only has the power to move,—
The Living Will. Whose Will, O God, but
    Thine?
Our minds are restless till they rest in Thee.

There, and there only, is the final Cause
And Origin of the world, the Last and First.
There, and there only is the secret found
Of that vast order which the astronomer
    saw
Ruling each atom as it rules the stars,
When to create and shape and paint one petal
In one brief April flower, a myriad atoms,

THE TORCH-BEARERS

Each atom in itself a universe
Of constellations, must in order climb
And wheel to their own stations in a scheme
Of intellectual beauty. The mind's eye
Can see them, radiant armies moving up
Through boundless night, to make one delicate
    point
Of colour, in a single wayside flower.
But O, what poet's hand on earth shall paint
    them?

    Up-whispered by what Power,
       Deeper than moon or sun,
Must each of the myriad atoms of this flower
    To its own point of the coloured pattern
         run;

    Each atom, from earth's gloom,
       A clean sun-cluster driven
To make, at its bright goal, one grain of
       bloom,
    Or fleck with rose one petal's edge in
       heaven?

THE LAST VOYAGE

What blind roots lifted up
This sacramental sign
Transmitting their dark food in this wild
  cup
 Of glory, to what heavenly bread and
  wine?

What Music was concealed,
 What Logos in this loam,
That the celestial Beauty here revealed
 Should thus be struggling back to its lost
  home?

Whence was the radiant storm,
 The still up-rushing song,
That built of formless earth this heavenly
  form,
 Redeeming, with wild art, the world's
  blind wrong;

Unlocking everywhere
 The Spirit's wintry prison,
And whispering from the grave, "Not here!
  Not here!

THE TORCH-BEARERS

He is not dead. The Light you seek is risen!"

But where, in this dissolving scheme, to pause
And read its meanings, where to halt and see
The picture of the cosmos? Is it here
On this world's coloured surface, in the scheme
That children know, of fields and flowers and birds
And kindly human faces? Is it there,
Along the dwindling road that Science treads,
Where flowers dissolve into electric mists,
And even the face of dying love dies out
Into a cloud of atoms. Better far
To walk with children through this present world,
Clear as a coloured picture-book, than lose
The light upon that face; for in God's mercy,
It may be that His best of meanings here
Lies nearest to us. Yet the mind runs back
Along those dwindling roads, explaining still
The greater by the less, until they reach
On every line of thought, that vanishing point

THE LAST VOYAGE

Where all runs out in absolute mystery.
There, at the last, seeking for that which *Is*
In its own right, and needs no other cause;
Where even the vanishing atom cries aloud
'I am, I am, yet have no right to be,'
(For only Nothingness ever had that right,
Except by that mind-shattering Miracle
Of ultimate Being,—the one impossible Fact
Which *is,* and lives, unfolding worlds on
    worlds
Where Nothingness might have been) there,
    Science meets
The fundamental paradox. . . .
Reaches the final contradictory crux
Where all its long descending roads must turn.
There stands the Gate, fine as a needle's eye,
Through which the mind must pass, and find
    the roads
Upon the further side of that strange point
Ascending, once again, to Thought and Will;
Ascending, till—as water finds its level—
It finds a height co-equal with the peaks
Of human thought; and infinitely higher,
Because that world beyond evolved our own;

THE TORCH-BEARERS

And we must find, upon the summits there,
A self-subsistent Cause, the eternal Fount
Of all that flowed into our world with Christ,
And showed us, in His Face, the Face of God.

Did His creation then, involve descent,
Renunciation, Sacrifice in Heaven,
A Calvary, at the very heart of things,
Wherein the Eternal Passion still enacts
In an eternal world what mortal eyes
Saw dimly on one shadowy hill of Time?

Once, once, ascending on those distant roads
Beyond our world, as in a dream, I came
Into a shining country, where I saw
A radiant throng, whose eyes in their clear
    depths
Held all the heavens of beauty, mirrored
    there
In ecstasy, as in a myriad pools
The splendour of the indivisible sun
Is mirrored, and the Godhead of all worlds
Descends and shines within a myriad souls,
In each a separate sacramental flame,

THE LAST VOYAGE

In each entire, the living form of God,
Super-substantial Life. They looked on me
And all that had seemed ghostly in their guise
Was now the very flesh and blood of life,
Firm as the ultimate forms of beauty and
    truth,
While all the things that I had touched on
    earth
Changed to intangible shadows. . . .
Then, as it seemed, the innermost Silence
    breathed,
More instantly than music through my soul,
The very voice of heaven,—*Be of good cheer.*
I have overcome the world.

                    I could not see
The Form that stood before me as I rose;
For this world's darkness like a midnight
    cloud
Still hid the eternal Splendour from these
    eyes;
But, at those words, a river of new strange
    tears
Dissolved my darkness into heavenly light,
And I beheld Him, not as eyes behold,

But as Love sees the light upon a face
Whereto the world is blind.

      I saw that Light;
And as a ship-wrecked man that would not
  breathe
His fear while danger threatens wife or child
Lest he should break their courage with his
  own,
But, when the peril is over, sobs out all,
My heart broke, crying dumbly, not in words,
All that dumb tears could speak,—
      "Blood on the way!
Blood on the way; Those agonies in the dark;
Cruelties; madness; evil setting its heel
On goodness; all the pangs, the desolate
  pangs
Of grief; the poor bowed head beside the
  grave;
Was there no way but this?"
      He looked at me,
And whispered, once again, "I *am* the Way."

Then, as a myriad flames will quiver and burn
In one rich jewel's blood-red heart, I saw

THE LAST VOYAGE

In His own wounded hands and feet and side
The wounds of all the world.

                    All the wild pangs
Of all earth's wars, all the red throes of Time,
All the long travail of Creation throbbed
Within those wounds. As in each rose on
    earth
Myriads of atoms, each a universe
Ordered to music move; wounds of the bird
Under the falcon's beak; wounds of the fawn
Under the tiger's fangs; wounds of mankind
Grappling in armies on that road of pain,
From earth's blind jungles up to Calvary's
    height;
Myriads of wounds; myriads of pangs were
    there;
Each like a separate flame within His
    wounds;
Rhythmical throes; not chaos now, not strife,
Not even grief as mortals think of grief;
But the strong music of the eternal Passion
Throbbing from hell to heaven in His own
    frame.
As the sea breaks in rhythm against its shores,

As the stars move in music through the sky;
As the heart throbs in man, all throbbed in
Him,
The eternal God made flesh, the Incarnate
Word,
The Logos of the evolving universe.
The iron of His world-ruling law was driven
By the strong doom of His world-ruling will
Through His own Body upon the eternal
cross
Of His creative sacrifice in heaven;
And dark as death on His death-conquering
brow
The whole world's thorns were woven to make
His crown.

XVI

About the break of day,
When the slow breakers of the Atlantic crum-
    bled
The crimson East through all their crests of
    foam,
I walked along the long wet shining deck
Breathing the salt strange freshness.
                  In the bows,
I saw a quiet throng, the throng I sought,
Bowing their heads to pass through a low
    doorway,
As though they knew their purpose, not as
    those
Who drift, but like strong swimmers to a goal
Through this world's idle fashion. As they
    entered,
And from their brows this outer daylight
    faded,
There was a strange new light on every face

[177]

As though they entered an unearthly chart-
    room
Wherein the secret splendour of our voyage
Must now be breathed to a few.
                       I followed them in,
And found them kneeling there before an altar
Spread with a linen cloth, whiter than snow,
(*Yea, though your sins be scarlet*—in my heart
The strange voice breathed,—*they shall be
    white as snow.*)
Lighted with candles, whose unwavering
    flames
Were of one order with those breathless fires
Which burn for ever in the Eternal City,
On earth, and in the heavens; and all were lit
From One Eternal Splendour, unto whom
All constellations burn; but here and now,
In little, those steadfast microcosmic fires
Held more significance for the mind of man
Than all the stars that move across the night
In their material order. Those twin flames
With that dark Crucifix, standing in the midst,
Of that pure altar, on the moving ship,
Marked but a moving shrine in one vast Fane;

THE LAST VOYAGE

And, as we moved, behind them I could see,
Through a broad window, the great heaving
    ocean
And the unmoving sky.
                    Wherever we moved
We moved not from the centre of that circle
Which had no bounds, and always held us
    there
Moving, yet motionless under the still regard
Of that all-seeing heaven.
                    I heard a voice
Breathing through Time in that now timeless
    tongue
Which, being what Death calls dead, can
    never die,—
Tuis fidelibus, Domine, vita mutatur. . . .
For unto Thy faithful, Lord, their life is
    changed
Not taken away; and their brief earthly abode
Being here dissolved, there is prepared an-
    other. . . .
Aeterna in coelis habitatio—
Eternal in the heavens.

        Therefore, with angels,
Archangels, Thrones, Dominions, and the host
Of the whole heavenly army without end
We hymn Thy glory.
        Sanctus, sanctus, sanctus,
Dominus Deus. Heaven and earth are full
Of Thy pure glory.
        Then the heights and depths
Met in one point,—I saw the host upraised,
Above the struggling sea, against the sky,
Gathering a million thoughts into one centre,
With all those cloud-like drifting earth-
    bound dreams
Of *Something far more deeply interfused*
Whose dwelling is the light of setting suns;
Closed in Reality now. That living Will
Whereby this coloured pageant of the world
In each material and electric atom
Is here and now sustained,—a myriad dreams
Brought to one lucid instance, one clear Fact
By that far Voice,—*In Memory of Me.* . . .
Brought to one present, living, personal Act,
By that far Will which, through the severing
    years,

Upraised that symbol, using mortal hands
Of flesh and blood, as His own instruments,
Through all those distances of Time and
      Space,
Here, now, to break that Bread and pour that
      Wine
Whereon He fed Who feeds us.
                    Time and Space
Dissolved. . . . Two thousand years ago, this
      Act
On earth (and in the heavens, before all
      worlds) ;
Foreshadowed His own passion to create,
Life that might share His own on high at last,
And, by His own transfiguring entrance here,
Ennoble the dark Nature He had made,
Stooping to Man, that men might rise to God.
There, as that host, upraised against the sky,
Bowed every head, I saw ten thousand shrines,
Ten thousand altars, in the salf-same Act
Made one, and shadowing forth that Act in
      heaven
Before which all those heavenly armies
      kneel. . . .

THE TORCH-BEARERS

All these and more made one by that one sign,
One thin white disk upraised against the sky,
There, in one strict concentring point at last,
Closed all the thoughts and aims of earth and
    heaven,
Shone the one signal that could never change,
The ultimate sea-mark of our voyaging souls.
Behind that Act, two thousand years ago
On earth, and in the heavens before all worlds,
Stood, and for ever stands, the eternal Christ,
Whose Presence is not separate from His Act,
Because, in Him, Substance and Will are one,
Breaking that Bread whereof His body was
    made,
In union and communion with man's own;
A sacramental sign, earth's common Bread,
Bread of a thousand grains, compact in one,
To feed that flesh wherewith the soul of
    Christ
Was clothed on earth, as man's own soul is
    clothed;
And, as the living soul of man on earth
Is here and now incorporate into Christ,
Becomes His Body anew.

THE LAST VOYAGE

           Time, Space, dissolved.
The eternal Logos, ordering the whole world,
The incarnate Word, in sacrament with man,
Breathed through Creation, with His instant
    voice,
Intelligible at last, as Love, not Death. . . .

*Now, and for ever, God makes heaven and
earth. . . .*

*Be of good cheer. I have overcome the
world. . . .*

I am the Resurrection, and the Life.

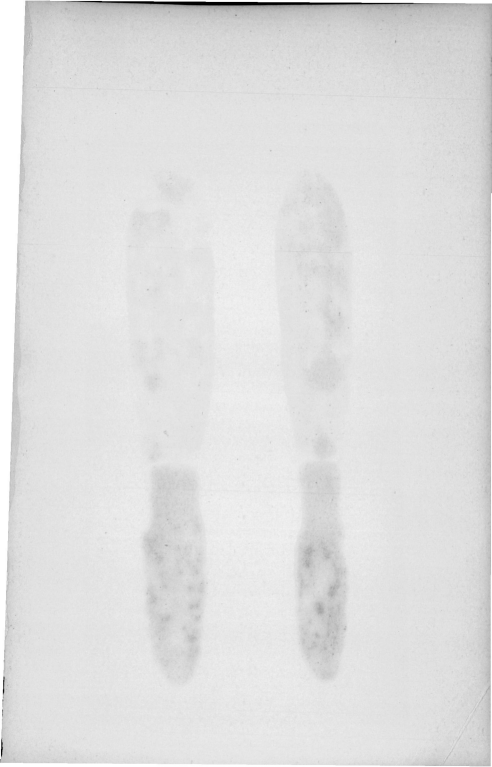

DATE DUE

GAYLORD   PRINTED IN U.S.A.